Contents

Introduction

Vocabulary

A Match.

1	Hello.	a	I'm twelve.
2	How are you?	b	My name's George.
3	What's your name?	c	I'm fine, thanks.
4	How old are you?	d	Hi.

B Match.

g n u a G v A M V F H Q U B h q C b j f O t N S D I c m R o Z i J K z P s T p d Y k L x X r E e l w W y

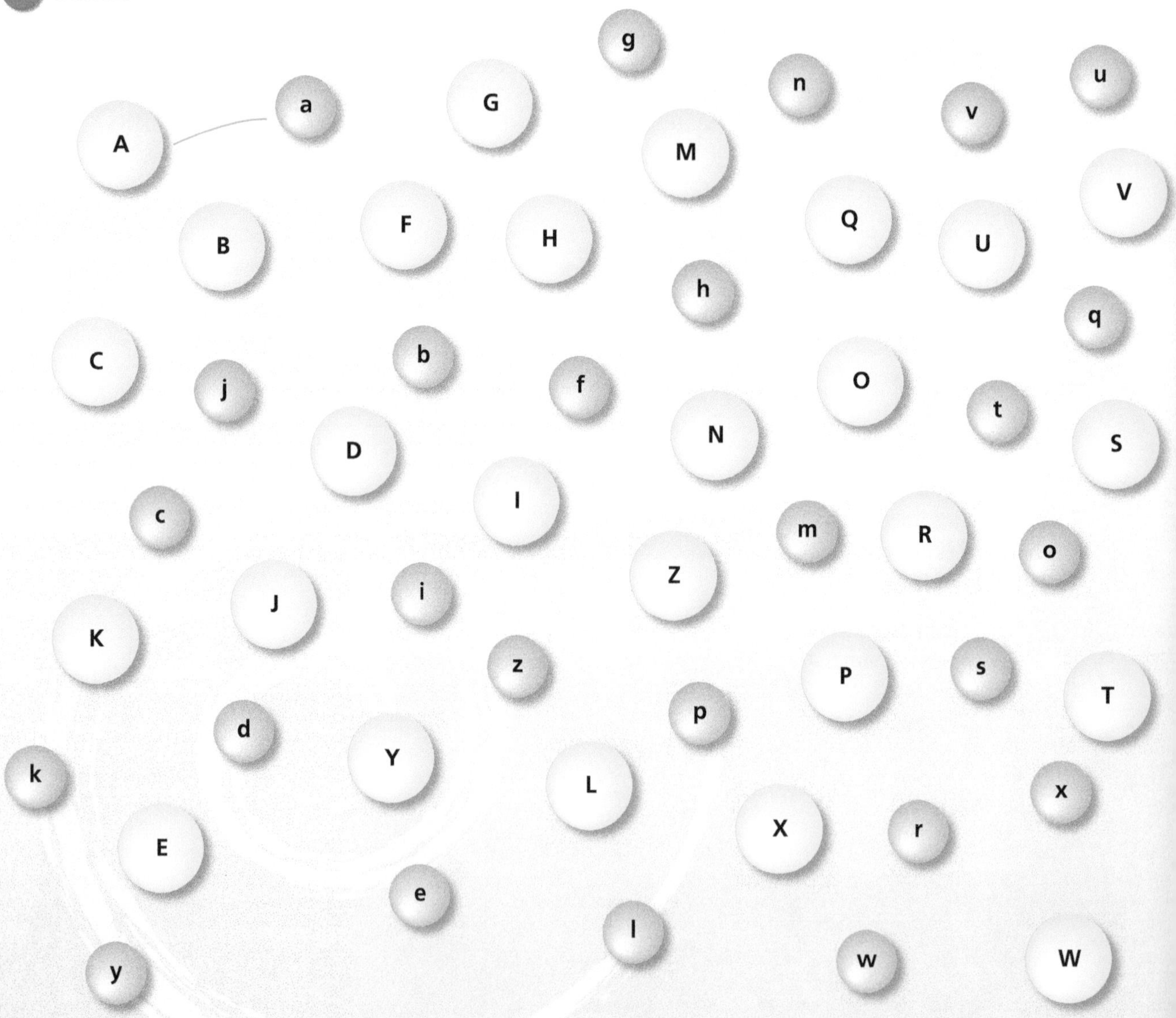

C **Find and write the days of the week, the months and the seasons.**

D	O	A	U	G	U	S	T	O	T	E	Q	N	R
E	K	U	M	E	P	A	U	E	V	J	O	F	O
C	P	T	U	N	S	D	E	B	S	A	U	S	A
E	S	U	Y	A	O	E	S	M	O	N	D	A	Y
M	A	M	O	A	R	X	D	A	L	U	C	T	B
B	L	N	L	P	B	Z	A	Y	K	A	E	U	C
E	A	N	F	R	E	O	Y	L	S	R	B	R	V
R	V	L	W	I	N	T	E	R	P	Y	E	D	O
E	N	O	F	L	W	O	A	B	L	V	S	A	P
T	O	C	T	O	B	E	R	P	J	U	L	Y	A
S	V	B	D	E	G	F	J	K	O	E	J	K	N
E	E	Q	S	U	V	A	X	L	S	B	F	A	W
P	M	A	R	C	H	E	F	L	U	P	E	S	E
T	B	R	N	K	S	P	R	I	N	G	B	O	D
E	E	J	F	A	U	V	I	A	D	P	R	S	N
M	R	A	G	K	M	K	D	L	A	E	U	P	E
B	K	P	H	A	M	I	A	V	Y	P	A	M	S
E	S	J	U	N	E	K	Y	A	O	E	R	Z	D
R	L	M	A	K	R	D	M	J	N	G	Y	F	A
U	V	S	P	Q	O	T	H	U	R	S	D	A	Y

Days of the week

Monday

Months

January

Seasons

summer

D Write the words.

1 5 → five

2 8 → ____________

3 17 → ____________

4 20 → ____________

5 33 → ____________

6 48 → ____________

7 50 → ____________

8 89 → ____________

9 100 → ____________

E Complete the sentences with these words.

answer mean open ~~please~~ spell

1 Can I use your pen, please?
Here you are!

2 How do you ____________ book?
B-O-O-K.

3 ____________ your books at page 38.

4 What's the ____________ to question 5?
I don't know.

5 What does *Wonderful World* ____________?

F Circle the correct words.

1 It's a / (an) umbrella.

2 These / This is a pen.

3 It's a / an hat.

4 Those / That books are red.

5 What's this / these?

6 It's a / an egg.

7 That's / Those a green bag.

8 It's a / an girl.

9 Those / This boys are bad!

10 It's a / an bird.

11 This / These pencils are black.

12 It's a / an ear.

G Complete the table.

Number	Word
1st	(1) first
(2) ____________	second
5th	(3) ____________
(4) ____________	eighth
10th	(5) ____________
(6) ____________	thirteenth
18th	(7) ____________
(8) ____________	twentieth
22nd	(9) ____________
(10) ____________	thirty-first

H Complete the crossword.

Across

2
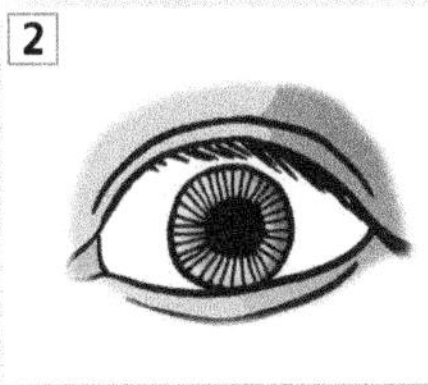

7
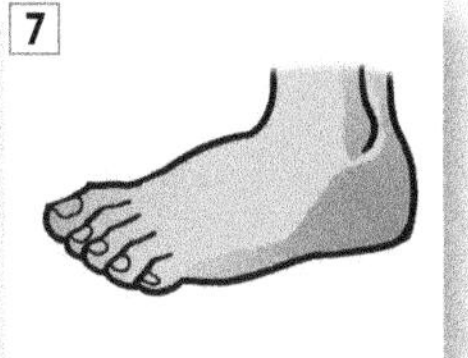

3

8
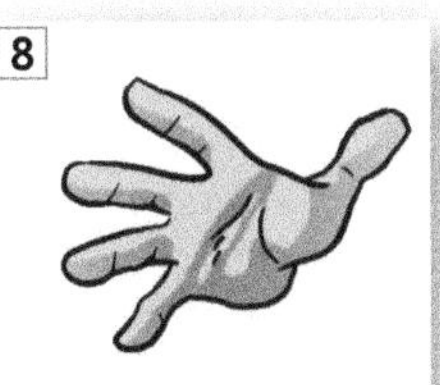

4
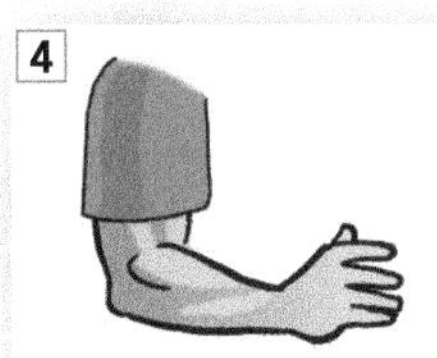

9
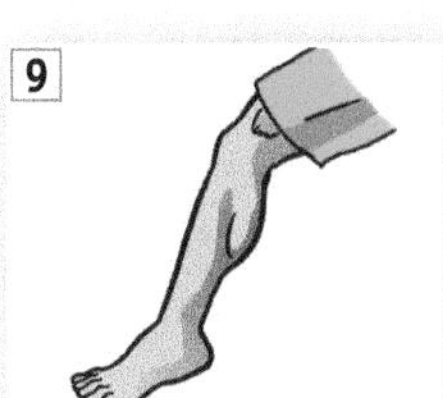

Down

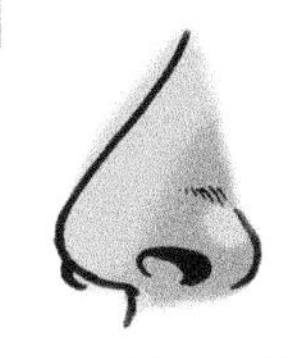

2
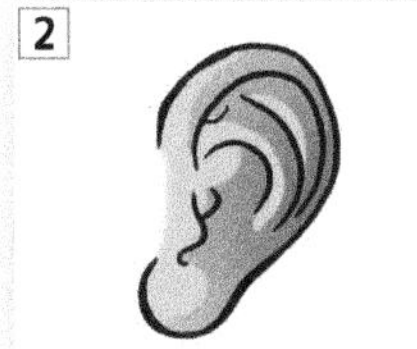

3
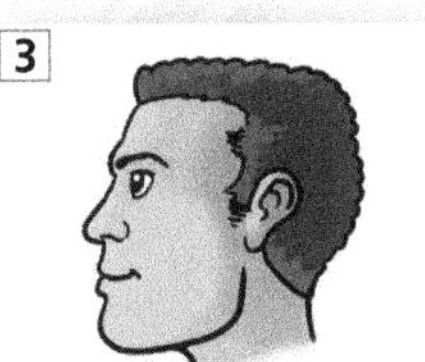

5
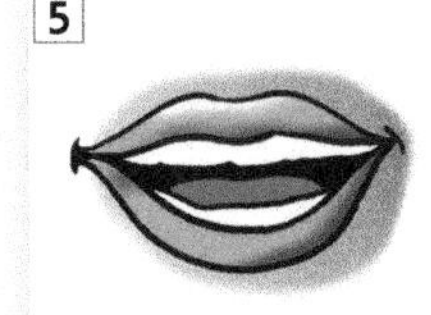

6
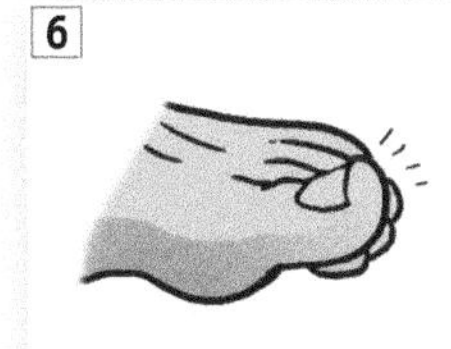

7
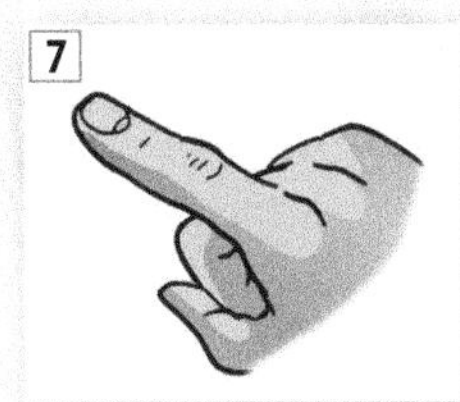

Introduction

1 **Complete the table with these words and their plurals.**

child country dog glass knife mouse tomato ~~toy~~

Singular	Plural
toy	toys

J Complete the times.

1

It's four o'clock.

2

It's ten to six.

3

It's half past twelve.

4

It's quarter past eight.

5

It's twenty-five past ten.

6

It's quarter to one.

7

It's ten to five.

8

It's nine o'clock.

9

It's quarter past seven.

K Colour the picture.

The pen is blue and the pencil is red. The book is black and the bag is orange. The clock is yellow and the desks are brown. The board is green and the door is purple.

Vocabulary

A Match.

a 
b 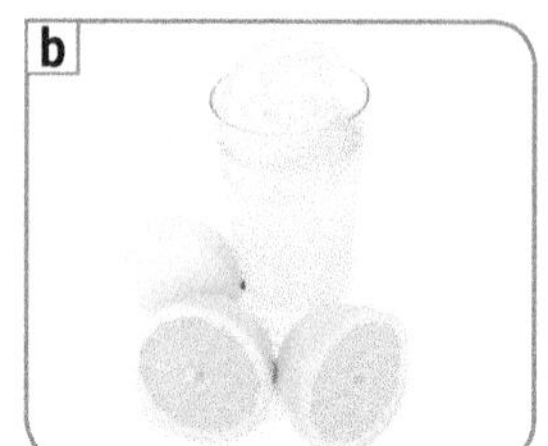
c 
d 
e 
f 
g 
h 

1 scientist [d]
2 beach [ ]
3 shark [ ]
4 friends [ ]
5 lemonade [ ]
6 house [ ]
7 family [ ]
8 idea [ ]

B Complete the sentences with these words.

black clever fair tall ugly young

1 My hair isn't dark. It's fair .
2 My cousin plays in a basketball team. He's ______ .
3 My sister is very ______ . She's two.
4 Mary isn't ______ . She's beautiful.
5 The shark isn't ______ . It's grey.
6 Good idea! You're very ______ .

C Match.

1 What's that?
2 Meet our friends, Kate and Robbie.
3 Hello. I'm Jake.
4 Uncle Oliver's a scientist.
5 What a stupid trick!
6 I'm sorry.

a Yes, very stupid.
b Hi! I'm Lily.
c Nice to meet you!
d It's a shark!
e It's OK.
f Really?

Grammar

A **Complete the sentences with am, are, or is.**

1 Mary ___is___ my sister.
2 I ________ on holiday.
3 Dan and Harry ________ funny boys.
4 ________ your mum a scientist?
5 ________ you here for the summer holidays?
6 You and I ________ cousins.

B **Circle the correct words.**

1 Hi! I'm / Am I Robbie.
2 Is / Are they old?
3 She aren't / isn't crazy about science.
4 Cool! We are / am on holiday.
5 The children aren't / isn't stupid.
6 It's / Is it a shark?
7 You're / Are you funny.
8 They are / is friends.

C **Choose the correct answers.**

1 Are Kate and Jake friends?
 a Yes, they are.
 b Yes, we are.
2 Are you ten years old, Tom?
 a No, you're not.
 b No, I'm not.
3 Is Betty your sister, Harry?
 a Yes, she is.
 b Yes, he is.
4 Children, are you crazy about summer holidays?
 a Yes, they are!
 b Yes, we are!
5 Is the boy tall?
 a No, he isn't.
 b No, it isn't.
6 Is the story funny?
 a Yes, they are.
 b Yes, it is.
7 Are you a student?
 a Yes, I am.
 b No, we aren't.
8 Is black your favourite colour?
 a No, it isn't.
 b No, they aren't.

Vocabulary

A Complete the paragraph with these words.

eat fly have keep live swim

Penguins (1) live in the Antarctic. They can't (2) ______. They (3) ______ in the sea. They (4) ______ one egg every year. Father penguins (5) ______ the eggs warm. They don't (6) ______ for two months! They get very hungry!

B Circle the odd one out.

1	cold	warm	stupid
2	father	mother	egg
3	parents	birds	penguins
4	amazing	cool	hungry
5	water	sea	son

C Find and write ten family words.

S	D	A	U	G	H	T	E	R	R	S
I	S	N	G	R	A	N	A	M	A	M
S	O	M	G	A	W	F	E	S	T	R
T	H	A	U	N	C	L	E	O	O	L
E	U	U	N	D	L	A	U	N	T	H
R	S	G	R	A	N	D	M	A	A	U
F	B	O	A	D	N	P	B	A	U	S
I	A	S	N	S	K	D	A	U	W	N
W	N	I	D	M	I	M	H	S	I	D
G	D	K	N	F	E	W	I	F	F	O
R	A	N	B	B	R	O	T	H	E	R

1 daughter
2 ______
3 ______
4 ______
5 ______
6 ______
7 ______
8 ______
9 ______
10 ______

Grammar

A **Match.**

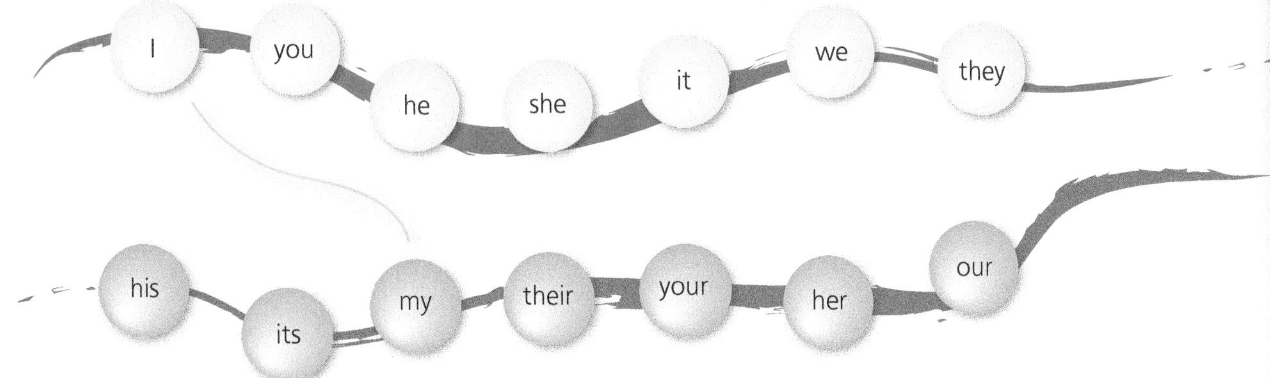

B **Circle the correct words.**

1 I / My live with my parents and my two brothers.
2 We / Our hair is black.
3 This is Maya. She / Her is 15 years old.
4 You / Your holiday photos are beautiful.
5 He / His isn't a tall boy.
6 Look at that cat! It's / Its ears are so small.
7 They / Their parents are scientists.
8 You're / Your very friendly.

C **Complete the sentences with these words.**

her his its my our their

1 This is John. ___His___ father is a scientist.
2 That's a funny cat. What's ____________ name?
3 Hi! I'm Rob and this is ____________ sister, Penny.
4 Aunt Carol is cool and ____________ husband is cool too.
5 Meet my friends. ____________ names are Will and Fred.
6 Paula and I are short and ____________ hair is fair.

Vocabulary

Complete the sentences with these words.

birthday class email matter twins

1 I've got one email .
2 Sasha is in ________ 2A.
3 The ________ are eleven years old.
4 'I'm sorry.' 'It's OK, it doesn't ________ .'
5 My ________ is on 8th May.

Grammar

Choose the correct answers.

1 ______ parrot is clever.
  a Grandmas
  b Grandma's
2 My ______ live in this house.
  a cousins'
  b cousins
3 Harry is my ________ friend.
  a brother's
  b brothers
4 The ______ names are Sarah and Andy.
  a childrens'
  b children's
5 Her ______ cat is black.
  a friends
  b friend's
6 What do ______ eat?
  a birds
  b bird's

Say it like this!

Match.

1 What's your name?
2 How old are you?
3 Where are you from?
4 When's your birthday?
5 What class are you in?

a I'm from Spain.
b I'm in Class 4A.
c My name's Thomas.
d I'm twelve years old.
e My birthday's on 7th October.

Writing

Remember!

A, B, C are capital letters.
Anna
. is a full stop.
We live in a house.
? is a question mark.
How old are you?
' is an apostrophe.
He's a tall boy.

A **Read Melissa's email and correct the punctuation.**

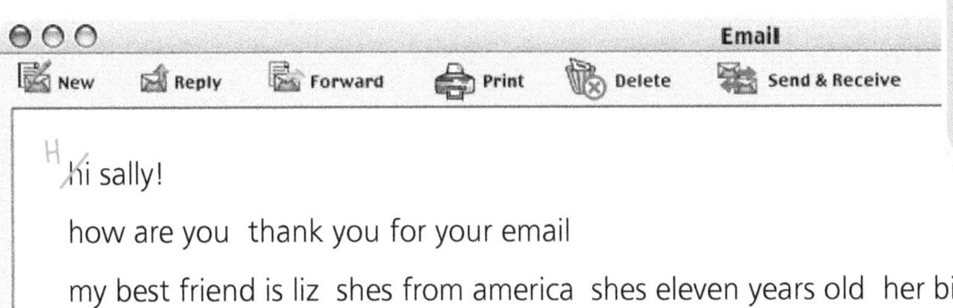

H
hi sally!

how are you thank you for your email

my best friend is liz shes from america shes eleven years old her birthday is on 25th january
she is crazy about cats

who is your best friend email me soon!

love,
melissa

B **Write an email about your best friend. Use the plan to help you.**

Begin like this:
Hi (your friend's name)!

How are you? Thank you for your email.

Answer the questions:
Who is your best friend?
Where is your best friend from?
How old is your best friend?
When is his/her birthday?
What is your best friend crazy about?

End like this:
Who is your best friend? Email me soon!

Bye for now,
(your name)

Email
New Reply Print Delete

Lesson 1

Vocabulary

A **Write the numbers next to the words.**

a	laptop	6
b	mobile phone	
c	teddy bear	
d	skateboard	
e	board game	
f	computer game	
g	lizard	
h	robot	

B **Look at the pictures and write the correct words or phrases.**

I don't know. ~~I'm scared!~~ Look! Please don't touch. Sorry! Welcome!

1 I'm scared!

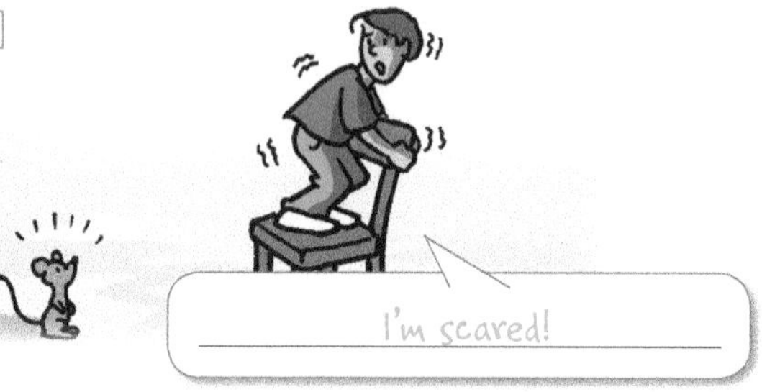

4 Where's that piece?

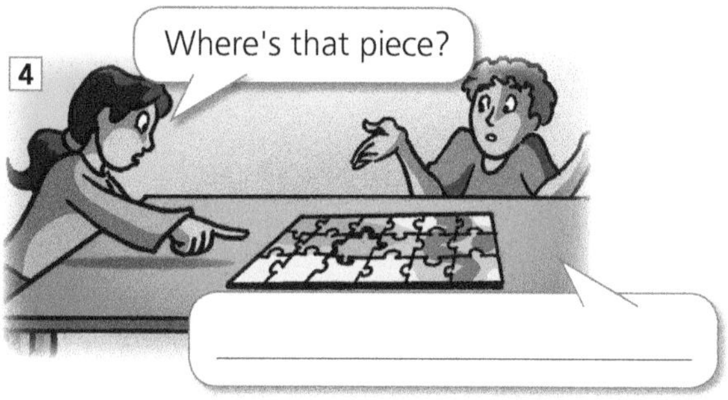

2

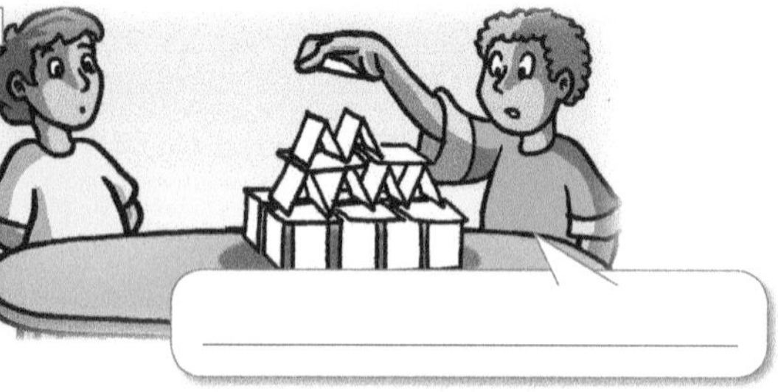

5 SMACK!

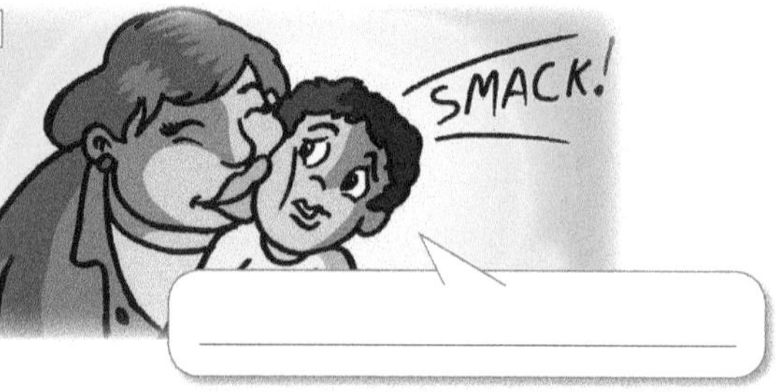

3

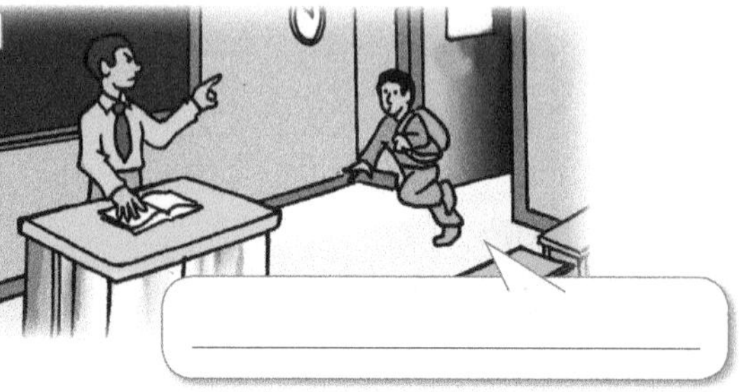

6

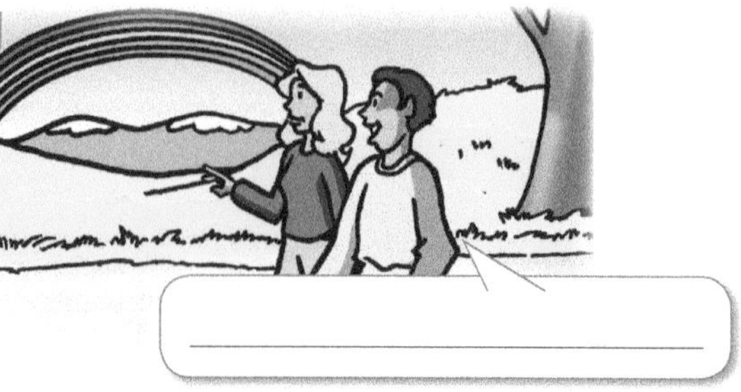

C **Complete the sentences with these words.**

bike message museum mystery pet picture pieces toys

1 Look at this _message_ on my mobile phone.
2 These are the baby's favourite ________ .
3 My dad isn't here. He's at the ________ .
4 What's the answer to the ________?
5 Wow! A new ________ . Can I ride it?
6 John's got a ________ lizard.
7 My new puzzle's got 1000 ________!
8 Don't touch that! It's my sister's ________ of Johnny Depp.

Grammar

A **Complete the sentences with have got or has got.**

1 My cousin _has got_ a new mobile phone.
2 That's my mum. She ________ fair hair.
3 Tony and Larry ________ cool bikes.
4 Alice ________ a lovely home.
5 I'm Joey. I ________ six sisters!
6 Where's the dog? It ________ my ball.

B **Circle the correct words.**

1 Pauline hasn't / haven't got a laptop.
2 They hasn't / haven't got a new computer game.
3 I like dogs but I haven't / have got a pet.
4 She's got / has got a lot of work.
5 That's my computer. Its / It's got a lot of good games.

C **Look at the pictures and write questions and short answers. Use have got or has got.**

1 Tom / a skateboard
Has Tom got a skateboard?
Yes, he has.

4 it / ears

2 Jane / a mobile phone

5 Paul / an uncle

3 they / pets

6 Mum and Dad / new car

Vocabulary

A Complete the sentences with these words.

camera DVD globe ice skates watch

1 I've got a new _watch_. I can tell the time.
2 You can see all the countries in the world on a ________ .
3 ________ are special shoes.
4 This is a great National Geographic ________ .
5 There are lots of photos in my ________ .

B Complete the crossword.

Across
1 These Batman ________ are very old.
3 Moon shoes are a great birthday ________ .
4 My ________ is on 12th July.
5 An astronaut walks on the ________ .

Down
1 Italy isn't a big ________ .
2 A tarantula is a big ________ .
3 He likes to play the ________ .

C Circle the correct words.

1 I'm scared of creepy / fast creatures.
2 It isn't a toy spider. It's real / strange!
3 I've got a lot of information / homework today.
4 Computer games are very exciting / strange.
5 I've got a toy spider with talking / moving legs.

Grammar

A Complete the sentences with the correct form of there is or there are.

1 Look! ___There is___ a spider on your desk!
2 Are you hungry? ______________ some apples in Oliver's bag.
3 ______________ any animals on the moon?
4 ______________ a map in the car?
5 I'm sorry but ______________ any lemonade.
6 No, ______________ any DVDs next to the laptop.

B Answer the questions.

1 Is there a computer in your classroom? ______________
2 Are there lots of toys in your room? ______________
3 Are there lots of people in your house? ______________
4 Is there a DVD in your bag? ______________
5 Is there a boy in front of you? ______________
6 Are there lots of children at your school? ______________

C Look at the picture and write sentences. Use There is or There are and prepositions of place.

1 tarantula / DVDs ___There is a tarantula in front of the DVDs.___
2 pen / globe and DVDs ______________
3 ice skates / piano ______________
4 boy / girl ______________
5 comics / desk ______________
6 laptop / desk ______________
7 lizard / laptop ______________
8 teddy bear / laptop ______________

Vocabulary

Complete the sentences with these words.

boring favourite fun guitar photo stories

1 Mark plays his _guitar_ in the evening.
2 This is my ________ board game.
3 I don't like to read ________ books.
4 My grandma tells us amazing ________ .
5 This is a ________ of our boat.
6 I have great ________ with my cat.

Speaking

My favourite thing!

Draw a picture of your favourite thing. Tell your partner about it.

Say it like this!

Look at the pictures and write the correct word or phrases.

Can I have a go? Catch! It's my turn! Slow down! Well done!

1 _Catch!_

2 ________

3 ________

4 ________

5 ________

Writing

A **Complete the sentences with and or but.**

Hello! My name's Brandon (1) ___and___ *my favourite thing is my skateboard!*

My skateboard is black (2) ________ *red. It's old* (3) ________ *it's fast. I keep it under my bed. My brother has got a skateboard too* (4) ________ *I never use it.*

I skateboard at the weekends (5) ________ *on Tuesdays when I haven't got a lot of homework. I like to go to the park. It's nice when I call my friends* (6) ________ *they come with me.*

I love my skateboard. I have great fun with it!

We use and to add something to a sentence.
We use but to show that something is different from another thing.

Mike and Sally are my friends.
I like computer games but I don't like board games.

B **Write about your favourite thing. Use the plan to help you.**

Begin like this:
Hello! Say your name. Say what your favourite thing is.

Answer the questions:
What colour is your favourite thing?
Is it old/new/fast/slow?
Where do you keep your favourite thing?
When do you use/play with your favourite thing?

End like this:
I love my (favourite thing). I have great fun with it!

Review 1

Reading

A Read the text about skateboarding.

Skateboarding is a lot of fun. It is a favourite hobby for kids in lots of countries. Some girls like skateboards. (1) ____. In some towns, all the boys have got skateboards.

Lots of kids ride their skateboards in the road. But it isn't a good idea because there are cars. (2) ____ In some towns there are skateboard parks near kids' houses. (3) ____ There are special ramps and you can skateboard very fast.

Skateboards are a good birthday present for young people. (4) ____ . There are lots of different skateboards in the shops. They have got cool pictures on them. (5) ____ Black and grey are in fashion at the moment.

So kids, try this hobby! Skateboarding is cool!

B Complete the text with these sentences.

a Skateboarding in the park is a good idea.

b But boys are crazy about skateboards!

c But they aren't good for very young children.

d The colours are great too.

e These parks are very exciting!

Vocabulary

Choose the correct answers.

1 Tom has got five computer ______ .
 (a) games
 b pieces

2 My ______ phone is white.
 a board
 b mobile

3 I'm scared of ______ .
 a friends
 b sharks

4 Sally's ______ is on 5th October.
 a birthday
 b country

5 This is a ______ of my bike.
 a comic
 b photo

6 Please don't ______ the toys.
 a touch
 b know

7 My aunt's husband is my ______ .
 a brother
 b uncle

8 Penguins can ______ very well.
 a talk
 b swim

9 The baby's ______ bear is on the bed.
 a teddy
 b lizard

10 I'm ______ I can't come to your party.
 a scared
 b sorry

11 ______! That cat is beautiful.
 a Look
 b Yuk

12 Do you want some ______?
 a idea
 b lemonade

Grammar

Choose the correct answers.

1 ______ they sisters?
 a Is
 (b) Are

2 Simon and Greg ______ got two cats.
 a have
 b has

3 'Is Sue tall?' 'No, she ______ .'
 a isn't
 b aren't

4 This is Mike. ______ dad is a teacher.
 a Her
 b His

5 Philip ______ got fair hair. He's got black hair.
 a haven't
 b hasn't

6 My ______ friends are funny.
 a brother's
 b brothers

7 They ______ got cool skateboards.
 a has
 b have

8 There ______ five books on the table.
 a is
 b are

9 Tom is ______ Alice.
 a next to
 b between

10 Elephants ______ small animals.
 a isn't
 b aren't

11 ______ dog is eight years old.
 a Our
 b We

12 Look! There ______ a spider in your bed.
 a is
 b are

3 Lesson 1

Vocabulary

A Find and write six school subjects.

M	A	T	S	A	M	A	R	R
G	E	O	G	R	A	P	H	Y
E	S	C	E	N	T	H	I	S
O	M	U	S	I	H	C	S	C
G	U	H	I	S	S	T	T	I
A	S	A	R	D	G	E	O	E
P	I	A	T	R	A	A	R	T
S	C	I	E	N	C	E	Y	A

1 geography
2 __________
3 __________
4 __________
5 __________
6 __________

B Circle the correct words.

1 My geography teacher / lesson is very nice.
2 What's the sum / answer to this question?
3 Today's day / date is Monday, 1st March.
4 '22 + 48 is 70.' 'Yes, well done / good luck.'
5 I use a calculator / machine for my maths homework.

C Complete the sentences with these words.

class football fun homework school subject

1 Art is my favourite subject .
2 I always have __________ with my friends.
3 They do their __________ in the afternoon.
4 The teachers at my __________ are very nice.
5 Sometimes we play __________ on Saturdays.
6 There are 20 children in his __________ .

Grammar

A **Look at the pictures and complete the sentences with these phrases. Use the Present Simple.**

brush her hair   play football   study English   teach maths   walk to school   wash the car

1 Jenny ___brushes her hair___ every day.

2 Jack ______________ on Sundays.

3 Evelyn ______________ in the morning.

4 Kevin ______________ at the weekend.

5 Mr Jones ______________ on Friday.

6 Mrs Brown ______________ on Thursdays.

B **Complete the paragraph with the Present Simple of the verbs in brackets.**

My little brother and I (1) ___go___ (go) to school at 8 o'clock. Mum (2) __________ (carry) my brother's bag, but I (3) __________ (like) to carry my bag. We (4) __________ (have) fun at school. My brother (5) __________ (play) games with his friends at break time. I (6) __________ (sit) under the trees with my best friends Annie and Clare. Clare (7) __________ (have) got a little brother too. He (8) __________ (do) his homework at break time!

C **Complete the sentences with at, every, on or in.**

1 I do my homework ___in___ the evening.
2 We play games in the park __________ the weekends.
3 __________ month Mum and Dad go to the cinema.
4 Tony has got a piano lesson __________ Wednesdays.
5 Janet watches TV __________ day.
6 My cousin goes to work at 6 o'clock __________ the morning.

Vocabulary

A Write the missing letters.

1 You play here at break time. p l a y g r o u n d
2 Books are kept in this room. l _ _ _ _ _ _
3 You wear this to school. u _ _ _ _ _ _ _
4 This is where you eat lunch at school. c _ _ _ _ _ _ _ _
5 These are children in your class. c _ _ _ _ _ _ _ _ _
6 You have this in your room for books. b _ _ _ _ _ _ _

B Circle the odd one out.

1	history	maths	(food)
2	teeth	slippers	shoes
3	fun	lessons	subjects
4	sport	music	homework
5	brush	clean	wear
6	spaghetti	classroom	burger

C Complete the sentences with these words.

carry clean ~~do~~ finish sing wear

1 We ____do____ seven subjects at school.
2 What time do you usually ________ school?
3 Do you ________ a uniform to school?
4 The teacher and pupils ________ the classroom after art.
5 We can't ________ all these books. We need a bag.
6 My little sisters ________ songs with their teacher.

Grammar

A Circle the correct words.

1 Kevin doesn't / don't like science.
2 Do / Does she do her homework after school?
3 I don't / doesn't play football in the playground.
4 Do your teachers gives / give you lots of homework?
5 Do / Doesn't Kelly and Georgina go to school?
6 Does Tom hasn't / have lunch at the cafeteria?

B Look at the picture and write short answers.

1 Do the pupils at this school wear uniforms?
Yes, they do.
2 Does the classroom have a bookcase?
____
3 Have the pupils got lots of books on their desks?
____
4 Do the pupils use calculators at this school?
____
5 Does the teacher look sad?
____
6 Do you like this classroom?
____

C Complete the dialogue with the Present Simple of the verbs in brackets. Use the negative or question form.

Lisa: Hi! My name is Lisa.
Sally: Hello! I'm Sally. I'm new at school. I (1) don't know (not know) much about Summerhill.
Lisa: Don't worry. I know everything! (2) ________________ (you / take) the bus to school?
Sally: No, I don't. I come to school in my dad's car.
Lisa: (3) ________________ (your father / work)?
Sally: Yes, he does, but he (4) ________________ (not work) in the mornings.
Lisa: (5) ________________ (you / like) sports, Sally?
Sally: Yes, I do. I love basketball.
Lisa: That's great, we can play together then. We (6) ________________ (not play) basketball during break time, but we like to play after school.
Sally: Sounds great!

Vocabulary

Match.

1 get — a breakfast
2 have — b up
3 do — c emails
4 send — d homework
5 go — e to bed

Say it like this!

Answer the questions.

1 How often do you go to the cinema?
____
2 How often do you read books?
____
3 How often do you wear a uniform?
____
4 How often does your mum use a computer?
____
5 How often does your friend come to your house?
____
6 How often do you play computer games?
____

Grammar

Look at the pictures and write T (true) or F (false).

1 

2 

3 

4 

5 

6 

1 Chris never gets up at 7 o'clock. F
2 We often do our homework before dinner. ☐
3 Mum always has breakfast. ☐
4 Nathan always gets 100% in tests. ☐
5 Our teacher sometimes gives us homework. ☐
6 Laura usually sends emails on Sundays. ☐

Writing

Adverbs of frequency show us how often we do something. They go before the main verb, but they go after the verb **be**.

We **usually** ride our bikes to school.
They are **often** at the park on Sundays.

A **Complete the text with the Present Simple of the verbs in brackets. Use the adverbs of frequency.**

Carmen's Day

Carmen (1) usually gets up (usually / get up) at 7.30 in the morning. She (2) ________ (always / have) breakfast with her mum and dad. Her mum drives her to school.

Carmen finishes school at 4 o'clock. She (3) ________ (sometimes / visit) her cousin Mike in the afternoon.

In the evening, Carmen (4) ________ (usually / do) her homework. Then she (5) ________ (often / send) emails to her friends. She goes to bed at 10.30.

B **Write about Paul's day. Use the pictures to help you.**

sometimes ✓ often ✓✓ usually ✓✓✓ always ✓✓✓✓

Paul usually gets up at 7 o'clock in the morning.

Vocabulary

A Match.

1 Dina reads comics. [e]
2 Charles goes swimming. [ ]
3 Stephen plays the guitar. [ ]
4 Martha goes ice-skating. [ ]
5 Sonya plays the piano. [ ]
6 Simon collects coins. [ ]
7 Kelly collects stamps. [ ]
8 Karim flies a kite. [ ]

B Circle the correct words.

1 Well done! You're the matter / winner.
2 This board game is boring. Let's watch / read a DVD.
3 We haven't got any Chinese / China money.
4 What do you collect / need from the shops, Mum?
5 Let's watch the kite competition / congratulations.
6 'I collect stamps.' 'Me / My too!'

C Complete the dialogue with these words.

Congratulations! Here you are. I'm happy! Me too! Thanks. ~~You're the winner.~~

Joe: This lesson is boring. I'm not happy.
Teacher: Joe Smith wins the story competition.
Joe: What?
Anna: (1) You're the winner. Well done!
Teacher: (2) ____________ Your story is fantastic, Joe. This book is for you. (3) ____________
Joe: Wow! (4) ____________
Teacher: OK, class. It's break time.
Anna: You're cool, Joe! How are you now?
Joe: (5) ____________
Anna: (6) ____________ We're all happy!

Grammar

A **Put the words in the correct order to make questions.**

1. ? / is / Doug's / what / hobby
   What is Doug's hobby?
2. ? / your / school / where / is
   ____
3. ? / kite / this / is / whose
   ____
4. ? / the / music / is / when / competition
   ____
5. ? / who / the / boy / clever / is
   ____
6. ? / favourite / is / thing / what / her
   ____

B **Answer the questions.**

1. Who's your best friend? ____________________
2. When is your English lesson? ____________________
3. What are your hobbies? ____________________
4. Where do you live? ____________________
5. What's your favourite game? ____________________
6. Where do you usually play? ____________________

C **Circle the correct words.**

1. What's / When's your favourite animal?
2. Whose / Who's the boy with the beautiful kite?
3. Where / When is the park?
4. Whose / Who's guitar is this?
5. When's / When is the next lesson?
6. What / Who is that girl?

Vocabulary

A Match.

a This film is boring.

b Let's send an email to Uncle Fred.

c I swim here on Saturdays.

d I'm hungry. Let's eat here.

e Let's go on the rollercoaster!

f Do you like the play?

1 theatre [f]
2 Internet café [ ]
3 restaurant [ ]
4 cinema [ ]
5 amusement park [ ]
6 sports centre [ ]

B Write the numbers next to the words.

a visitor [3]
b ferris wheel [ ]
c entrance [ ]
d slide [ ]
e merry-go-round [ ]
f rollercoaster [ ]

C Complete the sentences with these words.

face famous huge mirror scary tourist

1 This ride is very ___scary___. I don't want to go on it.
2 A ______________ is a visitor to a country.
3 This bike is ______________! I can't ride it!
4 Shakira is a ______________ singer.
5 I haven't got a ______________ so I can't look at my hair.
6 Look at his ______________ . He's got a big nose.

Grammar

A Circle the correct words.

1 A baby can / can't walk.
2 Birds can / can't fly.
3 Young children can / can't go on rollercoasters.
4 Grandpa can / can't run very fast – he's 80 years old.
5 Mum can / can't go on the children's rides.
6 I can / can't speak English.

B Write short answers.

1 'Can I go to the shops?' 'Yes, ___you can___.'
2 'Can John use your computer?' 'No, ______.'
3 'Can they play football?' 'No, ______.'
4 'Can Sandra go on the ferris wheel with me?' 'Yes, ______.'
5 'Can you make ice cream, Jack?' 'No, ______.'
6 'Can this dog go on the merry-go-round.' 'No, ______.'

C Complete the paragraph with can or can't.

My sister Daisy is ten years old. She likes music. She (1) ___can___ play the piano and she's very good at it. She likes the guitar too, but she (2) ______ play it. She wants to have guitar lessons. Mum says she (3) ______ have a lesson once a week. She (4) ______ have more lessons because she hasn't got time. Daisy plays the piano all the time. (5) ______ she finish her homework? Well, yes she (6) ______. I'm a good brother and I help her!

Lesson 3

Vocabulary

Complete the sentences with these words.

eat go help ~~like~~ meet play send visit

1 I ___like___ going to the park with my friends.
2 How often do you ________ your cousins?
3 Let's ________ swimming.
4 What time do you ________ your evening meal?
5 We don't phone our aunt. We ________ her emails.
6 Can you ________ me with my homework, please?
7 The boys always ________ football in the playground.
8 Dan and Sean ________ their friends at the sports centre.

Speaking

Tell your partner what you and your family like doing on Saturdays.

Say it like this!

Look at the pictures and complete the questions with Do you like or Are you good at.

1 ___Do you like___ swimming? — No, I don't.

2 ________ playing the piano? — No, I'm not.

3 ________ bowling? — Yes, I am.

4 ________ watching DVDs? — Yes, I do.

5 ________ skateboarding? — No, I'm not.

6 ________ going on the rollercoaster? — Yes, we do!

Writing

A **Complete the paragraph with these words.**

can   ~~is good at~~   likes   goes

My best friend's name is Emma. She's eight years old. Emma (1) ___is good at___ swimming and it's her favourite hobby. Emma (2) ______________ swimming with her friends every weekend. She swims at the sports centre near her house. Emma (3) ______________ swim very well. She (4) ______________ swimming because it's a sport and it's fun too!

Remember!

go shopping/ice-skating
like playing/reading
can speak/fly
be good at making/swimming

I go shopping at the weekends.
I like playing football with my friends.
I can speak French very well.
Mum is good at making cakes.

B **Write about your best friend's hobby. Use the plan to help you.**

Begin like this:
Say who your best friend is.

Answer the questions:
How old is your friend?
What's your friend's favourite hobby?
When does your friend do his/her hobby?
Is he/she good at it?
Why does your friend like his/her hobby?

Review 2

Reading

A **Read the text about learning to read and write.**

Ladybird SUNSTART Reading Scheme
On the beach

It is important to learn to read and write. It helps people learn about the world and it helps people find jobs. But some people don't know how to read a book or write their name. The problem is that in some countries children don't go to school. They want to go to school but they can't. Why is this? Well, they haven't got schools.

UNICEF wants to change this. UNICEF is the United Nations Children's Emergency Fund. It wants to help all children all over the world to go to school. UNICEF sends help to countries so they can open schools. We can help too. We can buy UNICEF notebooks and cards. The money goes to UNICEF and they use it to help children everywhere.

So next time you don't want to go to school, think about it. You are lucky to have a school, a teacher and books.

B **Circle the correct words.**

1 It is / isn't important to read and write.
2 Some countries haven't got schools / children.
3 UNICEF buys / helps schools.
4 Our money / notebooks can help UNICEF.
5 Teachers / Children are lucky to go to school.

Vocabulary

Choose the correct answers.

1 Mum usually has ______ in the morning.
  a restaurant
  (b) breakfast

2 Salma doesn't ______ her homework on Saturday.
  a do
  b make

3 My favourite subject is ______ .
  a bowling
  b science

4 Do you use a ______ for your maths homework?
  a calculator
  b rollercoaster

5 Harry never ______ his teeth!
  a wears
  b brushes

6 ______ from Japan often visit the Acropolis in Athens.
  a Classmates
  b Tourists

7 I want to go shopping but I haven't got ______ .
  a money
  b maths

8 You pay to get in the amusement park at the ______ .
  a entrance
  b harbour

9 Dad reads books from the ______ .
  a club
  b library

10 The ______ is Jan's favourite ride.
  a merry-go-round
  b theatre

11 Do you want to ______ TV?
  a watch
  b send

12 We can send emails at the Internet ______ next to the park.
  a coffee
  b café

Grammar

Choose the correct answers.

1 Dan likes history but I ______ geography.
  a likes
  (b) like

2 ______ you often go to the cinema?
  a Does
  b Do

3 I ______ pizza for dinner.
  a sometimes have
  b have sometimes

4 I'm ______ to see my aunt.
  a happy always
  b always happy

5 ______ jeans are these?
  a Whose
  b Who's

6 I ______ like art lessons.
  a don't
  b doesn't

7 ______ go bowling, Dad?
  a We can
  b Can we

8 Tracey can swim but she ______ ice-skate.
  a can
  b can't

9 ______ is the entrance to the school?
  a Where
  b When

10 ______ your sister like music?
  a Does
  b Do

11 Victoria ______ wear a uniform to school.
  a doesn't
  b don't

12 'Do you watch TV in the evening?' 'Yes, ______ .'
  a I don't
  b I do

Vocabulary

A **Put the letters in the correct order and write the party words.**

1 labnools balloons
2 keca ______
3 delscan ______
4 darc ______
5 tivnitonia ______
6 stensper ______

B **Circle the correct words.**

1 Let's get something from this paint / stall.
2 My dog can catch / throw a ball in his mouth.
3 It's very hot / quiet here. Where are all the people?
4 That's perfect. Good shot / turn!
5 Quick! / Ouch! My nose!
6 This festival / fight is beautiful.

C **Complete the dialogue with these words.**

Hey, you! Over there! Look! OK. This is fun! ~~What's that?~~

Tina: (1) What's that?
Ted: It's a paint stall. Let's get some paint for a fight.
Tina: (2) ______
Ted: (3) ______ They've got blue paint and red paint.
Tina: I like red – it's my favourite colour.
Ted: Let's throw paint!
Tina: Cool! (4) ______
Ted: Ouch! I've got green paint on my face!
Tina: It's that boy.
Ted: Where?
Tina: (5) ______
Ted: Oh, yes. (6) ______ Come back here!

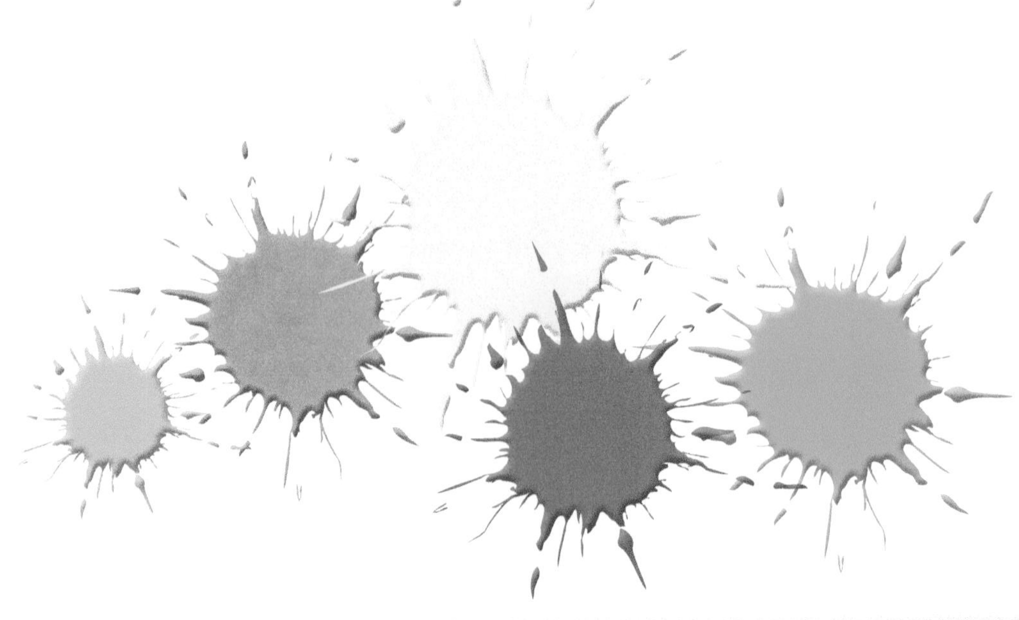

Grammar

A **Look at the pictures and complete the sentences. Use the imperative of these verbs in the affirmative or negative form.**

be catch clean eat go throw

B **Circle the correct words.**

1 There's the ball, Jack. Throw it / him!
2 Where's Mum? These presents are for her / them.
3 We / Us like going to festivals.
4 Here are your friends. Let's give you / them some cake.
5 Have we got any paint? Yes, these colours are for us / it.
6 It's Dad's birthday. Let's buy her / him something nice.
7 Tony, please phone me / you from the festival.
8 She / Her has a party every year.

C **Match.**

1 It's seven o'clock in the morning.
2 We're hungry.
3 I like games.
4 The festival starts in ten minutes.
5 We've got a test.
6 It's Grandpa's birthday.

a Let's have a paint fight.
b Let's get up.
c Let's study.
d Let's get him a present.
e Let's have lunch.
f Let's be quick.

Vocabulary

A Find and write eight carnival words.

A	M	A	S	F	C	A	B	T
P	M	A	G	I	C	I	A	N
A	F	I	I	R	E	W	C	W
P	I	R	T	E	C	B	O	P
A	R	I	T	W	O	O	S	I
R	W	C	L	O	W	N	T	R
A	O	W	B	R	B	C	U	A
D	M	A	S	K	O	O	M	T
E	M	A	K	S	Y	H	E	E

1 magician
2 ______
3 ______
4 ______
5 ______
6 ______
7 ______
8 ______

B Choose the correct answers.

1 The ______ lives with the king.
a clue
(b) queen

2 Let's go on a treasure ______ .
a ride
b hunt

3 Lots of people ______ at the carnival.
a burn
b dance

4 Fred likes making models out of ______ .
a paper
b masks

5 Look at the ______ snowman – it's huge!
a secret
b giant

6 Do lots of people ______ part in the carnival?
a wear
b take

C Complete the sentences with these words.

city ~~hat~~ king person preparations street

1 Dad wears a funny ___hat___ on his head at every carnival.
2 The ______ with the best costume is the winner. I hope it's me!
3 Paris is a lovely ______ .
4 The name of my ______ is Hatton Gardens.
5 The ______ for the carnival take months.
6 Peter goes to the carnival as a ______ every year.

Grammar

A Complete the tables with these words.

B Choose the correct answers.

1 I made ten party ______ with Mum's help.
 a hat
 b hats

2 I send them ______ New Year card every year.
 a a
 b –

3 The ______ at the party was very good.
 a food
 b foods

4 Tom has got ______ new computer games.
 a two
 b a

5 We always buy nice ______ for our friends.
 a present
 b presents

6 'What are you doing Lucy?'
 'I'm writing ______ invitation.'
 a an
 b a

7 There were a lot of new ______ in the box.
 a CD
 b CDs

8 I always have ______ fun at my friends' parties.
 a a
 b –

C Look at the pictures and complete the sentences with countable or uncountable nouns.

1 Tanya has got five ___balloons___ .
2 Heather has got beautiful long ______________ .
3 Mr Brown makes amazing ______________ for the carnival.
4 Sam drinks ______________ every morning.
5 Monkeys eat ______________ at the Monkey Party.

Vocabulary

Complete the sentences with these words.

~~give~~ have laugh light make open play sing

1 I hope Mr Smith doesn't ___give___ us a test.
2 I always __________ jokes on my brother.
3 I want to __________ a cake for my birthday.
4 Do you __________ songs at weddings?
5 Please __________ the candles on the cake.
6 Dad's jokes are very funny and we always __________ at them.
7 At birthday parties, we __________ presents.
8 My grandparents and I __________ a meal together every Sunday.

Grammar

Complete the dialogue with some or any.

Clare: Happy Birthday, Lynn!
Lynn: Thanks, Clare. Guess what! Mum says I can invite (1) ___some___ friends to my house for a birthday party.
Clare: That's great! We can listen to music at the party. Have you got (2) __________ CDs?
Lynn: Yes, but I haven't got (3) __________ good ones.
Clare: Don't worry. I've got (4) __________ great CDs. We can listen to those.
Lynn: Oh dear! I haven't got (5) __________ invitations.
Clare: It doesn't matter. You can phone your friends.
Lynn: That's a good idea. I love parties.
Clare: Me too! Let's make (6) __________ party food!

Say it like this!

Look at the pictures and make suggestions. Use Why don't you...? and these phrases.

have a party have a picnic go to an Internet café ~~go to bed~~ go to the doctor

1 ___Why don't you go to bed?___

2 __________

3 __________

4 __________

5 __________

Writing

A **Circle the correct words.**

New Year
(Lian, 9, China)

New Year's in China is great! On New Year's Eve we all help to clean the house and Mum cooks. (1) She / Her always cooks fish and chicken. Families decorate their living rooms with beautiful flowers and fruit. (2) They / Them also write happy things on red pieces of paper and stick (3) they / them on the walls. Children always go to bed late on New Year's Eve. (4) We / Us like to watch the fireworks. They are amazing! On New Year's Day, everybody visits friends and family. I wear red clothes and Dad takes a picture of (5) I / me. My clothes are usually new. New clothes bring good luck for the New Year!

Remember!

We use reference words when we don't want to repeat the same noun. Subject and object pronouns are good reference words.
The children are dancing. They are happy.
I've got a new costume. Do you like it?

B **Write about a special day in your country. Use the plan to help you.**

Answer the questions:
What is the special day?
What does each person in the family do?
What is important on this day?
What do you like to do on this day?
What do you wear on this day?

6 Lesson 1

Vocabulary

A Match.

a

b

c

d

e
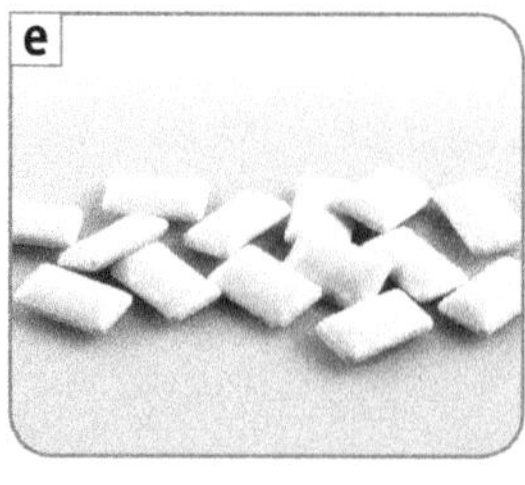

f

1	burger	c	4	cheese	
2	sandwich		5	ketchup	
3	tomato		6	chewing gum	

B Complete the sentences with these words.

bill delicious fast hungry menu waiter

1 Let's get something to eat at this ____fast____ food restaurant.
2 This is a ________________ meal. Thanks.
3 Let's look at the ________________ . What? £200!
4 Mum, we're ________________ . When is lunch?
5 There are lots of nice meals on this ________________ .
6 Can you ask the ________________ for some water, Dad?

C Write D (Drink), F (Food) or O (Object).

1	orange juice	D	5	water	
2	dessert		6	chips	
3	plate		7	table	
4	glass		8	cake	

Grammar

A Circle the correct words.

1 This fast food restaurant has got lots of / much different burgers.
2 There isn't many / much orange juice. Let's buy some more.
3 My cat drinks a lot of / much water.
4 There aren't many / much people at the restaurant.
5 I don't eat many / a lot of fast food.
6 Are there many / much snacks on this menu?

B Put the words in the correct order to make sentences.

1 this / aren't / dessert / oranges / in / there / many
There aren't many oranges in this dessert.
2 got / haven't / I / many / plate / on / my / chips
____
3 there / on / spoon / ice cream / isn't / my / much
____
4 restaurant / that / has / got / waiters / many
____
5 table / are / lots / snacks / of / on / the / there
____
6 always / cat / my / food / a lot of / eats
____

C Complete the sentences with How much or How many.

1 How many people are at the restaurant?
2 __________ water do you want?
3 __________ are these tomatoes?
4 __________ children want orange juice?
5 __________ food do we need for the party?
6 __________ sandwiches have you got?

Vocabulary

A **Find and write ten things you can eat.**

C	H	O	C	O	L	A	T	E
H	P	O	H	A	P	P	L	A
E	M	R	I	C	E	P	B	B
E	C	H	C	B	C	P	R	A
S	H	M	K	U	H	L	E	P
E	I	M	E	A	T	E	A	P
B	B	A	N	A	N	A	D	L
B	U	T	T	E	R	H	M	E
S	P	A	G	H	E	T	T	I

1 chocolate
2 ______
3 ______
4 ______
5 ______
6 ______
7 ______
8 ______
9 ______
10 ______

B **Complete the sentences with these words.**

answer ~~holes~~ leaves letters luck

1 Swiss cheese has got lots of holes in it.
2 There are 26 ______ in the English alphabet.
3 What's the ______ to question 5?
4 Some people can read tea ______!
5 In England black cats are good ______ .

C **Complete the dialogue with these words.**

~~cup~~ health knife milk plate slice Swiss

Mum: Do you want a (1) cup of hot tea?
Dad: No, thanks. I've got a glass of cold (2) ______ here.
Mum: Well, have a (3) ______ of cheese for your sandwich.
Dad: Yum. It's (4) ______ cheese. My favourite! Can I have an apple for dessert? It's very good for your (5) ______ .
Mum: Yes, I know. Here you are. Do you want this (6) ______ to cut the bread?
Dad: Yes, please. I also need a (7) ______ to put my sandwich on.
Mum: Here you are.
Dad: Thank you!

Grammar

A **Choose the correct answers.**

1 Are there ______ fast food restaurants here?
 a a little
 (b) lots of

2 Can I have ______ water, please?
 a a few
 b a little

3 Gary wants ______ chocolate, but Mum says no!
 a lots
 b lots of

4 Can I have ______ chips with my burger?
 a a few
 b a little

5 Sorry, we haven't got ______ milk.
 a a lot of
 b little

6 There are ______ menus on that table.
 a a few
 b a little

B **Match.**

1	We've got a	a	lots of chips on my plate.
2	Yum. I've got	b	little orange juice?
3	Can I have a	c	a few more sandwiches.
4	Have you got	d	lot of apples.
5	Do you want	e	a lot of chocolate?
6	Darren always takes a	f	few apples to school.

C **Circle the correct words.**

1 Dad drinks a (little) / few milk for breakfast.
2 Let's have a lots / lot of food at the party.
3 Jane eats little / lots of chocolate.
4 Can you buy me a few / few apples?
5 The cat drinks a few / lots of water in the summer.
6 Greg likes a lot / little mustard in his sandwich.

Vocabulary

Circle the odd one out.

1 dessert snack restaurant
2 dish meal slice
3 different popular cool
4 small big little
5 plates pizzas frogs' legs
6 cook eat make
7 biscuits rice crepes
8 fish chips tea

Speaking

Food in my country!

Write a list of the food that is popular in your country. Tell your partner about your favourite food.

Say it like this!

Complete the dialogue with these words.

favourite food how often love they're horrible what about

James Hunt
Fruit: ✓
Eggs: ✗
Favourite food: burgers and chips
When: Saturday

Reporter: James, what's your (1) favourite food?
James: I (2) ________ burgers and chips.
Reporter: (3) ________ do you eat burgers and chips?
James: Every Saturday.
Reporter: Do you like fruit?
James: Yes, I do.
Reporter: (4) ________ eggs?
James: No, (5) ________ .

Writing

Remember!

First, then, after that and finally are time words. We use them to show the order of events.
First, we wash the apples.
Then/After that, we cut them into slices.
Finally, we put them on a plate with lots of ice cream.

A **Complete the paragraph with these words.**

After   Finally   First   Then

My favourite place to eat is Joe's Restaurant. We always go there on Saturdays with my mum and dad. (1) ___First___, we have a drink. (2) __________, we have pizza and some spaghetti with tomato sauce. Dad always asks for more cheese on his spaghetti. My brother doesn't have any spaghetti. He prefers pizza. (3) __________ that, we have some dessert. My brother and I have ice cream with biscuits and fruit. (4) __________, my parents have coffee. We always have a wonderful meal at Joe's Restaurant!

B **Write about your family's favourite place to eat. Use the plan to help you.**

Begin like this:
Say where your favourite place to eat is.

Answer the questions:
When do you go to this place?
What do you eat/drink first?
What do you eat after?
What do you have for dessert?

End like this:
Say why it's your favourite place to eat.

Review 3

Reading

A **Read about food for kids.**

Do you eat a snack at school? What do you usually buy? Do you like fruit, or do you want chocolate?

Lots of kids buy food at school, and guess what? They choose things that aren't good for them. It isn't strange. Kids like burgers, chips and ice cream. They don't want oranges, bananas or rice. This is a problem. When kids eat fast food every day it is bad for them. They sleep in lessons. They don't do sport. They feel tired.

But lots of kids want to learn about healthy food. It's easy! Make a delicious chicken sandwich with tomatoes and cheese. Now that's a healthy snack! Try fruit in small pieces with some juice. It's a great dessert!

Then why not have a delicious burger or pizza one day a week? Fast food is OK, but don't eat it every day.

B **Write T (true) or F (false).**

1 Kids buy healthy food at school. F
2 Kids don't usually choose fruit at school. ☐
3 It isn't good to eat fast food very often. ☐
4 Kids don't want to know about healthy food. ☐
5 You can eat fast food once a week. ☐

Vocabulary

Choose the correct answers.

1 Where is my ______ to the party?
   a menu
   (b) invitation

2 Jackie's queen ______ is great.
   a biscuit
   b costume

3 Do you eat ______ every day?
   a paint
   b meat

4 Sandwiches are delicious ______ .
   a snacks
   b clues

5 How many ______ are there on the cake?
   a cowboys
   b candles

6 That restaurant has got very good ______ .
   a waiters
   b festivals

7 I need a ______ to cut the chicken.
   a knife
   b cup

8 ______ are beautiful at night.
   a Parades
   b Fireworks

9 The ______ is very good at moving things.
   a treasure
   b magician

10 Do you want some ______ on your bread?
   a dessert
   b butter

11 Can I have the ______, please?
   a bill
   b Chinese

12 It's my birthday ______ on Saturday.
   a party
   b joke

Grammar

Choose the correct answers.

1 Let's ______ lunch now. I'm hungry!
   a to have
   (b) have

2 ______ eat all the bread. I want some too.
   a Don't
   b Doesn't

3 Only ______ adults like this fast food restaurant.
   a a few
   b a little

4 Grandma always gives ______ clothes at Eid.
   a me
   b her

5 Stan loves ______ and he eats it every day.
   a a rice
   b rice

6 Can I have some ______? They're my favourite fruit.
   a banana
   b oranges

7 There's ______ food in the kitchen for lunch.
   a a
   b some

8 How ______ candles are there on the cake?
   a many
   b much

9 A ______ of people like spaghetti.
   a few
   b lot

10 There's the waiter. Can you give this money to ______?
   a him
   b it

11 How ______ does the meal cost?
   a many
   b much

12 They haven't got ______ costumes in this shop.
   a some
   b any

7 Lesson 1

Vocabulary

A Match.

a 
b 
c 
d 
e 
f 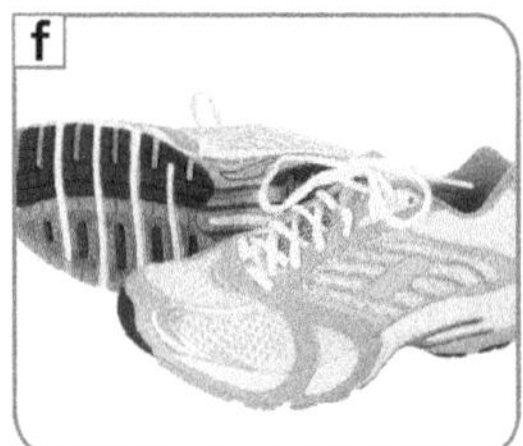
g 
h 

1 finishing line [e]
2 trophy [ ]
3 park [ ]
4 picnic [ ]
5 referee [ ]
6 runner [ ]
7 trainers [ ]
8 spoon [ ]

B Circle the correct words.

1 Do you want to put / enter the competition?
2 My brother can cross / win the finishing line before you!
3 Does Jack often fall off / out his bike?
4 When the referee says 'Get ready, set, run / go!' you start the race.
5 Come / Look on, Steve! Let's go and play.
6 Stop it and push / leave us alone!

C Write the missing letters.

1 You do this on a horse. r i d i n g
2 You need good boots for this. c _ _ _ _ _ _ _ _
3 Can you ride a bike? Then this is for you. c _ _ _ _ _ _ _
4 Are you fast? Put on your trainers and show me. r _ _ _ _ _ _ _
5 Come with me on my boat and we can do this. s _ _ _ _ _ _ _
6 Wear your mask and let's find some fish! d _ _ _ _ _ _

Grammar

A Complete the table.

Verb	Present Continuous
play	I am playing
come	you ______
run	he ______
lie	she ______
swim	it ______
chase	we ______
have	you ______
cross	they ______

B Choose the correct answers.

1 Tom and Jim ______ playing football.
a am
(b) are

2 Dad's ______ with Uncle John at the moment.
a cycling
b is cycling

3 Look at Harry. He ______ the race.
a is winning
b winning

4 Oh no! My dogs ______ chasing that cat.
a am
b are

5 She's ______ a picnic with her friends in the park.
a have
b having

6 We ______ in our new trainers.
a are running
b is running

7 I ______ on my bed at the moment.
a am lying
b lie

8 You ______ your new trousers.
a is wearing
b are wearing

C Look at the pictures and complete the sentences. Use the Present Continuous of these verbs.

chase fall off have ~~run~~ swim win

1 He is running very fast.

2 They ______ together.

3 Joanna ______ the egg and spoon race.

4 I ______ my cousin.

5 We ______ breakfast.

6 Mike ______ his skateboard.

Vocabulary

A Complete the table.

Sport	Person
gymnastics	gymnast
boxing	
football	
tennis	
cycling	
swimming	

B Complete the sentences with these words.

feel get kick love think train ~~use~~ want

1 In Thai boxing you ___use___ your hands and legs.
2 How many hours a day does a gymnast ______________?
3 In football, you can ______________ the ball.
4 You've got a tennis lesson so please ______________ ready.
5 I ______________ to be a cycling champion.
6 My friends often ______________ excited before a football game.
7 You want to win so don't ______________ about anything else.
8 In Thailand the boys ______________ Thai boxing.

C Circle the correct words.

My cousin Max is a great tennis player. He (1) practises / helps three times a week after school. He takes part in competitions and he often (2) wins / makes prizes. Before a match, he is (3) sad / calm because he really wants to play well. Sometimes, he doesn't win but he never (4) gives up / falls off. I feel very (5) fat / excited when he plays in competitions and I always watch him. I think he's a (6) champion / wrestler!

Grammar

A **Rewrite the sentences in the negative form of the Present Continuous.**

1 I'm pushing my sister.
I'm not pushing my sister.

2 You're winning the game.

3 He's thinking about the fight.

4 She's wearing a helmet.

5 It's chasing birds.

6 We're watching cycling on TV.

7 You're feeling excited about the race.

8 They're giving up!

B **Put the words in the correct order to make questions.**

1 ? / playing / you / football / are
Are you playing football?

2 ? / your / is / training / brother

3 ? / calm / feeling / are / you

4 ? / is / him / chasing / dog / the

5 ? / you / practising / are / at / moment / the

6 ? / her / Julia / is / homework / doing

C **Look at the picture and write short answers.**

1 Are Carl and Alan playing tennis?
No, they aren't.

2 Is Angela cycling?

3 Is Rex chasing a ball?

4 Is Ted riding a bike?

5 Are Sylvia and Sophie climbing?

6 Is Missy running?

Vocabulary

Complete the sentences with these words.

coach competition country film skater work

1 My sister wants to be an ice ___skater___ .
2 Our football ___ helps us train.
3 Ice-skating is hard ___ .
4 These champion boxers are from the same ___ .
5 What's the name of your favourite ___?
6 The winners of the ___ get a great prize.

Say it like this!

Complete the dialogue with these words.

fan like match player team

Maya: Do you (1) ___like___ football?
Alice: Yes, I love football!
Maya: Who's your favourite football (2) ___?
Alice: I'm a Wayne Rooney (3) ___!
Maya: I like him too but I prefer Cristiano Ronaldo.
Alice: And which is your favourite football (4) ___?
Maya: I'm a Manchester United fan.
Alice: Me too! Let's go to a football (5) ___ together.
Maya: That's a great idea!

Grammar

Look at the pictures and write sentences. Use the Present Continuous.

1 Kate / tonight
Kate is doing her homework tonight.

2 Mr Brown / on Tuesday
___

3 Eric and Phil / this evening
___

4 Patty / tomorrow
___

5 Betty and Alex / at weekend
___

6 Danny / next week
___

Writing

Remember!

Tomorrow, this evening, next week, at the weekend, at the moment, in a month etc are time expressions. They are used with the Present Continuous to talk about future plans.

Tomorrow, I'm going swimming with my friends.

A **Read the email and answer the questions.**

Email

New Reply Forward Print Delete Send & Rece

Dear Jason,

How are you? It's Thursday and I've got a lot of things to do this weekend. Tomorrow, I'm playing tennis with my friend Jake in the morning. In the afternoon, I'm going shopping with my dad and in the evening I'm helping Mum cook dinner. On Saturday, I'm doing my homework in the morning. After lunch, I'm swimming at the sports centre.

What are you doing this weekend?

Write back soon,

Salim

1 When is Salim playing tennis? Salim is playing tennis on Friday morning.
2 When is he going shopping with his dad? ______________________
3 When is he helping his mum cook dinner? ______________________
4 When is he doing his homework? ______________________
5 When is he swimming? ______________________

B **Write an email to a friend about your plans for the weekend. Use the plan to help you.**

Begin like this:
Dear (your friend's name),
How are you?

Answer the questions:
Have you got a lot of things to do this weekend?
What are you doing Friday morning/ afternoon/evening?
What are you doing Saturday morning/ afternoon/evening?

End like this:
What are you doing this weekend?
Write back soon,
(your name)

Email

New Reply Print Delete

8 Lesson 1

Vocabulary

A **Complete the paragraph with these words.**

hand	hear	live	piece	work

This is my flat. I (1) ___live___ here with my mum and dad. My grandparents come here every day because my parents (2) ________ from nine in the morning to five in the evening. Listen! I can (3) ________ them now on the stairs. 'Hi, there! What's that in your (4) ________, Grandma? Yum, it's chocolate! Can I have a (5) ________ now, please?'

B **Find and write eight different homes.**

T	O	W	E	R	S	I	G	L
R	U	T	O	W	E	G	U	C
E	S	A	C	O	T	L	E	O
O	E	C	A	S	T	O	C	T
H	O	U	S	E	B	O	A	T
U	F	L	T	A	L	T	S	A
T	L	F	L	A	T	A	L	G
S	O	G	E	I	G	L	E	E
E	T	H	O	U	S	E	H	O

1 ___tower___
2 ________
3 ________
4 ________
5 ________
6 ________
7 ________
8 ________

C **Circle the correct words.**

1 Oh, no! The knight / bedroom is chasing us.
2 I think someone's coming. I can hear stairs / footsteps.
3 The view / trick from here is beautiful.
4 Help! I can see a monster / family!
5 This house is 200 hands / years old.
6 How many people / places live in these flats?

Grammar

A **Complete the sentences with the Present Simple or the Present Continuous of the verbs in brackets.**

1 My cousin ___lives___ (live) in London.
2 Please be quiet. I ______ (watch) TV.
3 ______ you ______ (like) houseboats?
4 Daisy ______ (not go) to school on Saturdays.
5 We ______ (want) to visit the castle.
6 ______ Mum ______ (eat) dinner at the moment?
7 He always ______ (play) with his friends at the weekends.
8 I ______ (not do) my homework now.

B **Match.**

1	Does she	a	like your jokes.
2	Are you	b	listening to music?
3	John doesn't	c	sees her grandma.
4	Mary often	d	live in a cottage?
5	Kate is	e	they making an igloo?
6	Are	f	watching a film.

C **Look at the picture and complete the text. Use the Present Simple or the Present Continuous of these verbs.**

be eat hold not like visit wear

At the moment, Tom and his mum (1) ___are visiting___ a castle. The castle (2) ______ 800 years old. Look! There's Tom's mum. She is (3) ______ a blue coat. She is coming down the stairs. Tom's mum is scared because she (4) ______ the old stairs. She thinks they are dangerous. Where is Tom? Oh, there he is! He's next to a knight. What (5) ______ the knight ______? Hee hee! It's a red umbrella. Tom isn't scared. He's very happy because he (6) ______ an ice cream.

8 Lesson 2

Vocabulary

A **Put the letters in the correct order and write the jobs.**

1 tipol pilot
2 traco ______
3 redshariser ______
4 tintsed ______
5 rtgfierefih ______
6 codrot ______
7 axti rdvire ______
8 phos saisntats ______

B **Circle the correct words.**

1 John and Bill work in the same / different office.
2 When I make / get sick, I sleep all day.
3 I get up / on early for school every day.
4 Do you like sleeping in a tent / fire?
5 'Is your job hard / easy?' 'Yes, it's very difficult.'
6 Dan makes / checks a fire every morning.
7 Look at that cowboy! He is getting on / in his horse.
8 Mum cooks / gives breakfast every morning.

C **Write the numbers next to the words.**

a cowboy [4]
b cows [ ]
c fire [ ]
d grass [ ]
e breakfast [ ]

Grammar

A Read the sentences and write T (true) or F (false).

1 You mustn't do your homework. F
2 Doctors must help sick people. ☐
3 Children must drive cars. ☐
4 Boxers mustn't fight. ☐
5 We must be quiet in the classroom. ☐
6 Cowboys mustn't ride horses. ☐

B Read the note and complete the sentences with must or mustn't.

I'm working this evening.
Please do these things for me.
Jack – cook spaghetti
Toby – clean your shoes, give the cat its medicine
Thanks,
Dad
PS No computer games and no TV!

1 Dad ___must___ work this evening.
2 Jack ______ cook spaghetti.
3 Toby ______ clean his shoes.
4 Toby ______ give the cat its medicine.
5 Toby and Jack ______ play computer games.
6 Toby and Jack ______ watch TV.

C Match.

1 It's a school day. — d
2 You're sick.
3 The dog is hungry.
4 Adel has got a maths test.
5 They don't feel well.
6 I've got lots of homework.

a We must give it some food.
b He must study.
c They must go to the doctor.
d We must get up early.
e I mustn't watch TV.
f You mustn't go to school.

Vocabulary

Match.

1 play e
2 lake
3 dinosaur
4 garden
5 church
6 capital

Say it like this!

Complete the dialogue with these questions.

Can you go swimming?
Is it a big city?
What can you do there?
What's it like?
~~Where do your cousins live?~~

Julie: (1) Where do your cousins live?
Adam: In Barcelona.
Julie: (2) ______
Adam: It's great.
Julie: (3) ______
Adam: Yes, it is.
Julie: (4) ______
Adam: You can go to the museums or eat at nice restaurants.
Julie: (5) ______
Adam: Yes, you can. There are beautiful beaches in Barcelona.

Speaking

Tell your partner about the different things you can do in your city.

Writing

We use because to explain the reason for something. We use so to explain the result of something.

I'm going to bed now because I'm tired.
I feel sick so I'm not going to school today.

A **Complete the postcard with because or so.**

Hi Liz!

Montreal is beautiful! My uncle's house is beautiful too. I have my own room (1) because my cousin is studying in London. We're having a great time! My uncle works, (2) __________ I go shopping with my aunt. We don't go for walks (3) __________ it's very cold. In the evening, we all have dinner together. I'm going to bed soon (4) __________ I must get up early tomorrow. We're going ice skating!

Write to me soon!

Amani

Liz Smith
7718 Ball St
Manchester,
England.

B **You are on holiday. Write a postcard to a friend. Use the plan to help you.**

Begin like this:
Hi (your friend's name)!

Answer the questions:
Where are you?
Is it nice there?
Where are you staying?
What can/can't you do there?
What are you doing tomorrow /at the weekend?

End like this:
See you soon!
(your name)

....

....

....

....

....

....

....

....

....

Review 4

Reading

A **Read about sailing.**

Sailing is a great sport and you can start when you are very young. Most children start sailing from the age of seven or eight. There are usually two groups for children at sailing schools. The first is for children aged eight to twelve years old, and the second is for children aged twelve to sixteen years old. A few sailing schools have lessons for children aged four to seven.

A lot of schools give a lesson on what to do before the students actually get on the boats. Most schools have special shoes for students, but the students must bring their own towels and warm clothes.

The lessons can last 30 minutes or 2 hours. There are also lessons which children can do in the holidays. So how much does sailing cost? Well, it is expensive. The lessons can cost from £20 a lesson to £200 or more.

B **Write T (true) or F (false).**

1 Most children start sailing from the age of four. F
2 Schools give their students special shoes. ☐
3 Students must bring their own towels. ☐
4 All lessons last two hours. ☐
5 Lessons can cost £20 or more. ☐

Vocabulary

Choose the correct answers.

1 Henry's favourite sport is ______ .
  (a) boxing
  b boxer

2 We are scared because it is very ______ in the castle.
  a dark
  b knight

3 Janet is a ______ and she trains every day after school.
  a diving
  b gymnast

4 The footballer ______ the ball and scores.
  a kicks
  b pushes

5 John wants to enter the sailing ______ .
  a champion
  b competition

6 Paris is the ______ of France.
  a capital
  b cottage

7 Go up the ______ carefully.
  a stairs
  b lakes

8 I'm going shopping ______ with Annie and Brenda.
  a yesterday
  b tomorrow

9 We have nice teeth because we visit the ______ every six months.
  a doctor
  b dentist

10 You must be strong to go ______ .
  a footballer
  b climbing

11 My ______ has got two bedrooms.
  a trophy
  b flat

12 We want to go ______ but the sea isn't calm.
  a ice-skating
  b sailing

Grammar

Choose the correct answers.

1 We ______ playing football at the moment.
  a is
  (b) are

2 ______ you practising for the race?
  a Am
  b Are

3 I usually ______ for two hours on Friday.
  a train
  b am training

4 We ______ get up early because our school is far away.
  a must
  b mustn't

5 A swimmer must ______ a lot.
  a train
  b training

6 Kathy ______ in a tennis competition next Saturday.
  a plays
  b is playing

7 'Are you cooking breakfast?' 'No, ______ .'
  a I am
  b I'm not

8 ______ George live in that house?
  a Is
  b Does

9 Do you often ______ to the hairdresser?
  a going
  b go

10 You ______ go to bed late when you've got school in the morning.
  a must
  b mustn't

11 Lucas and Bob ______ looking at the view.
  a aren't
  b isn't

12 ______ Pauline playing tennis at the moment?
  a Is
  b Are

9 Lesson 1

Vocabulary

A Match.

1 Excuse — a course.
2 No, — b please.
3 Of — c me.
4 Be — d on.
5 Come — e careful.
6 Yes, — f thanks.

B Choose the correct answers.

1 The ______ on the bus were very nice.
(a) seats
b water

2 I can't take lots of clothes to the hotel because my ______ is small.
a suitcase
b passport

3 You must use ______ on the beach.
a milk
b sun cream

4 My ______ is black.
a hotel
b rucksack

5 I don't like hotels, so I take a ______ with me on holiday.
a goat
b tent

6 I like your new ______ .
a hat
b village

C Complete the dialogue with these words.

camel ~~desert~~ hot pyramid sand thirsty

Bob: What are you looking at, Tina?

Tina: It's a photo from my holiday. We're in the (1) desert . That's me – I'm riding a (2) ______ . They can walk well on (3) ______, you know.

Bob: Cool! Is that huge building a (4) ______?

Tina: Yes. And look, there's my dad.

Bob: He looks very (5) ______ . His face is all red.

Tina: I know. He's drinking water because he is (6) ______ .

Grammar

A Circle the correct words.

1 We was / were in France last week.
2 There / They were lots of tourists at the castle.
3 Our holiday last month / Month ago was great.
4 Was George / George was at the beach yesterday?
5 'Was Jim at home?' 'No, he was / wasn't.'
6 Was / Were your holiday photos nice?
7 I was at the pyramids three days ago / last.
8 There wasn't / weren't many people at the hotel.

B Look at the pictures and write questions and short answers. Use the Past Simple of Be.

1 be / the hotel nice
Was the hotel nice?
No, it wasn't.

4 be / Alice hot

2 be / the tourists happy

5 be / Henry excited

3 be / the leopard scary

6 be / his climbing boots new

C Answer the questions.

1 Were you at school yesterday? ______
2 Where were you last Saturday? ______
3 How many children were there in your class last year? ______
4 Was your friend at your house last week? ______
5 Was your last holiday fun? ______

9 Lesson 2

Vocabulary

A Complete the word groups.

chicken inventor land pilot ship station

1 bus, plane, ship
2 sheep, duck, ________
3 passenger, flight, ________
4 scientist, invention, ________
5 go up, travel, ________
6 port, airport, ________

B Complete the sentences with these words.

air basket farmer field get smoke start tie

1 Passengers travel in a basket under a hot air balloon.
2 You must ________ running in the morning. It's great for your health.
3 The plane was up in the ________ for three hours.
4 Look at that ________ ! Is there a fire?
5 Let's ________ something red on the suitcase so we can find it at the airport.
6 The first hot air balloon landed in a ________ .
7 A ________ has got animals like chickens and cows.
8 Some people ________ married in hot air balloons.

C Choose the correct answers.

1 They ____ animals on the first hot air balloon flight.
a used
b landed

2 I saw the Queen ____ England last week.
a off
b of

3 I wait at the bus ____ for ten minutes every morning.
a platform
b stop

4 The first hot air balloon was in the ____ for only a few minutes.
a bottle
b air

5 What's your ____ name?
a first
b finally

6 They ____ the bag with smoke.
a scared
b filled

Grammar

A Complete the table.

Verb	Past Simple
live	(1) lived
(2) ______	carried
look	(3) ______
(4) ______	cooked
(5) ______	tried
need	(6) ______
use	(7) ______
(8) ______	played

B Complete the sentences with the Past Simple of the verbs in brackets.

1 He wanted (want) to go for a ride in a hot air balloon.
2 We ______ (travel) to Damascus by plane.
3 They ______ (look) for a nice hotel.
4 Janet ______ (stop) travelling last year.
5 Everyone ______ (like) the holiday.
6 Katy and John ______ (study) all weekend for the test.
7 I ______ (talk) for hours at the party.
8 Mr Stevens ______ (watch) the tennis match on TV.

C Circle the correct words.

1 They started school last / in month.
2 I visited my grandparents in August / year.
3 Dad cooked chicken tomorrow / yesterday.
4 Rozier travelled in a hot air balloon in / on 1783.
5 We stayed in Muscat for three weeks two years last / ago.
6 Stewart played football next / last weekend.

Vocabulary

Choose the correct answers.

1 I need lots of money in Paris because it's a very ______ city.
  a interesting
  (b) expensive

2 Let's go ______ on our bikes.
  a running
  b cycling

3 The food here is ______ .
  a exciting
  b delicious

4 My brother is at the ______ . He's flying to Oman in an hour.
  a airport
  b plane

5 We always ______ to Rome by car.
  a travel
  b ride

6 I don't like cheap ______ because the rooms are small.
  a hotels
  b tents

Grammar

Complete the sentences with the Past Simple of the verbs in brackets.

1 Last year, we __went__ (go) to New York and we __had__ (have) a great time.
2 She ______ (do) a lot of shopping on Saturday and she ______ (wear) her new clothes to the party.
3 Last month, Paula ______ (get) married and everyone ______ (buy) her lovely presents.
4 We ______ (sit) at the table and we ______ (eat) burgers and chips.
5 They ______ (take) their swimsuits on holiday and they ______ (swim) every day.
6 Mum ______ (see) Uncle George at the shops and she ______ (tell) him to visit us.

Say it like this!

Look at the pictures and answer the questions.

5

1 How does Stephanie get to work?
  Stephanie goes to work by taxi.
2 How does Jason get to school?
  ______
3 How do the Taylors go shopping?
  ______
4 How does Alex get to the park?
  ______
5 How does Jenny get to her grandparents?
  ______
6 How do the girls get to their friend's house?
  ______

Writing

Adjectives describe nouns. We use adjectives before nouns and after the verb **be**.
Samantha has got a **new** dress.
Natasha is **beautiful**.

A **Read the text and underline the adjectives.**

I went to Berlin with my family two months ago. Berlin was beautiful! We went by plane and stayed in an amazing hotel. It was big with a swimming pool and a gym.

We did lots of exciting things in Berlin. We got up early every day and went for long walks. The parks in Berlin are huge. At night, we usually ate in nice restaurants. The food was delicious!

We stayed in Berlin for ten days. We had a great time! We also met some friendly people. Berlin is a fantastic place to visit!

B **Write about a city that you visited. Use the plan to help you.**

Answer the questions:
Where did you go?
What was it like?
Where did you stay?
What did you do there?
Where did you eat?
How long did you stay?
Is it a nice place to visit?

10 Lesson 1

Vocabulary

A Complete the sentences with these words.

acting interview lines pop group stage

1 Tony sings in a pop group .
2 I watched a(n) ____________ with Julia Roberts yesterday.
3 Sam is learning his ____________ for the school play.
4 The director said my ____________ was very good.
5 At the end of the play, all the actors get on the ____________ .

B Circle the correct words.

Last week, my class went on a school trip to a film (1) studio / stage. It was very exciting. We saw them (2) shoot / cut some of a film. I talked to a (3) costume / cameraman and he told me about his job. He was very (4) funny / pretty and he made me laugh. Then, an actor gave me his (5) audience / autograph. He is a great actor and he's got a lot of (6) concert / talent. It was a great day!

C Complete the crossword.

Across

2 The actor's costume is in his ____________ room.
4 I went to the Robbie Williams ____________ and it was great!
6 Hurray! I've got a ____________ in the school play.

Down

1 Stephen Spielberg is a famous film ____________ .
3 I love singing and I want to be a ____________ one day.
5 Stop watching TV please because dinner is ____________ .

Grammar

A **Complete the sentences with the negative form of the Past Simple. Use the verbs in bold.**

1 We **saw** a concert on TV, but we ___didn't see___ a film.
2 The actors **wore** their costumes, but they ______________ their shoes.
3 The director **liked** her acting, but he ______________ her singing.
4 The cameraman **had** his bag, but he ______________ his camera.
5 Bill **gave** me a DVD for my birthday, but he ______________ me a CD.
6 We **went** to the theatre last night, but we ______________ to a restaurant.

B **Answer the questions.**

1 Did you have breakfast this morning? ______________
2 Did you eat spaghetti last night? ______________
3 Did your teacher give you a test yesterday? ______________
4 Did you see a play last week? ______________
5 Did you go on holiday in July? ______________

C **Look at the answers and complete the questions.**

1 Which ___film did Jenny like___?
Jenny liked *Toy Story 3*.
2 When ______________?
I saw the play last week.
3 What ______________?
We ate spaghetti.
4 What ______________?
Mark brought his camera.
5 Where ______________?
They went to the Bahamas.
6 Why ______________?
They left because they were tired.

10 Lesson 2

Vocabulary

A Complete the advert with these words.

adventure comedy ~~dream~~ love make musical

Work in Films!

Do you (1) dream of fame?
Do you want to (2) ______ lots of money?
Then you can work in films!

Are you funny? Try a (3) ______ .
Can you sing? A (4) ______ is for you.
We find roles in (5) ______ films too.

This is a job we all (6) ______ .
It's great!

B Choose the correct answers.

1 He started a film ______ .
a character
(b) company

2 Some people are ______ . They don't have a lot of money.
a poor
b famous

3 Mickey Mouse is famous all ______ the world.
a about
b over

4 Talented actors win ______ .
a pictures
b Oscars

5 The film company didn't ______ any money.
a make
b do

6 My dad keeps his car in the ______ .
a studio
b garage

C Write P (Person) or F (Film).

1 adult P
2 cartoon
3 child
4 drama
5 neighbour
6 science fiction
7 visitor
8 horror

Grammar

A Complete the questions with a question word.

1 '___When___ did you get to the cinema?'
'I got there at nine o'clock.'

2 '________ was your mum?'
'She was fine.'

3 '________ did you buy?'
'I bought a ticket for the play.'

4 '________ did they shoot the film?'
'They shot it in Jordan.'

5 '________ did you talk to?'
'I talked to your sister.'

6 '________ did you study all day yesterday?'
'Because I've got a test today.'

7 '________ action film did you prefer?'
'I preferred *Transformers*.'

8 '________ did you get to work?'
'By bus.'

B Read Peter's diary and answer the questions.

Sunday, 12th June
I went to the beach today and I saw my friends. I swam all morning in the sea. I ate a burger and an ice cream, but the ice cream wasn't nice. Then I was cold, so I went home in the afternoon. In the evening, I felt very tired! Now, It's 10 o'clock and I'm going to bed.

1 Where did Peter go? ___He went to the beach.___
2 When did he go? ________
3 What did he do in the morning? ________
4 Which food did he prefer? ________
5 Why did he go home? ________
6 How did he feel in the evening? ________

C Match.

1 Which actor was in the film?
2 When did you go to the theatre?
3 How did you get home after the party?
4 Why did John go home early?
5 Who invented Mickey Mouse?
6 Where did Mark buy the DVDs?

a Walt Disney.
b By taxi.
c Angelina Jolie.
d At the supermarket.
e On Sunday.
f Because he was tired.

Vocabulary

Choose the correct answers.

1 She has got ______ every day.
   (a) lessons
   b musicals
2 I'm ______ about horror films.
   a crazy
   b hard
3 I want you to write a film ______ for homework.
   a story
   b review
4 I had a(n) ______ for the musical last week.
   a joke
   b audition
5 I must ______ my lines for the play.
   a practise
   b sing
6 Who is your favourite ______ in the film *Shrek 3*?
   a subject
   b character
7 Try and ______ before the audition.
   a feel
   b relax
8 I was very ______, but I did OK.
   a difficult
   b nervous

Say it like this!

Complete the dialogue with these words.

about amazing favourite great ~~singer~~ songs

Phil: Who's your favourite (1) __singer__?
Simon: I'm crazy (2) ______ Justin Timberlake. He's an (3) ______ singer!
Phil: Can you dance to his (4) ______?
Simon: Yes, they're wonderful! And who's your (5) ______ singer, Phil?
Phil: I'm crazy about Kanye West. He's (6) ______!

Speaking

Tell your partner about your favourite film. Talk about the actors and the story.

Writing

A Complete the text with the topic sentences.

A Johnny Depp was born in the USA.
B Johnny Depp acts in many films.
~~C Johnny Depp is my favourite actor.~~
D Johnny Depp is a great actor.

Paragraphs separate a piece of writing into different parts. The first sentence of each paragraph introduces the topic of the paragraph. This sentence is called a topic sentence. Each paragraph has got a different topic sentence.

My Favourite Actor

(1) __C__ . His birthday is on 9th June. He is very famous because he is in many popular films. He is funny and clever. He is also a very good actor.

(2) ______ When he was young he wanted to be a musician in a group. Although he played at a few important concerts with famous singers, in the end he decided to become an actor.

(3) ______ His most famous films are *Edward Scissorhands*, *Pirates of the Caribbean* and *Charlie and the Chocolate Factory*. My favourite one is *Charlie and the Chocolate Factory* because children and adults can watch it.

(4) ______ He can play many different characters. Sometimes he is funny and sometimes he is scary. That's what I like about him. Johnny Depp is my favourite actor because he has got a lot of talent.

B Write about your favourite actor. Use the plan to help you.

Paragraph 1: Say who your favourite actor is and why.
Paragraph 2: Write about his/her life when he/she was a child.
Paragraph 3: Write about his/her most famous films.
Paragraph 4: Say why you think he/she is so talented.

Review 5

Reading

A **Read about a holiday in Egypt.**

Three of our readers went on holiday to Cairo last May.

Sami

I had a great time. The Pyramids were a bit boring and I didn't like the camels. But the hotel was great! I swam in the pool and I played football every day with some kids from France.

Dina

The hotel was very nice. The rooms were big and the food in the restaurant was delicious. I was amazed because the Pyramids were next to the hotel! The view from my room was fantastic.

Will

I got sick, so I wasn't happy for a few days. I got bored at the hotel. At the end of the week we visited the Pyramids. They were huge! Then I rode a camel. I was scared at first but it was a very calm animal. I really liked my day in the desert.

B **Write S (Sami), D (Dina) or W (Will).**

Who…

1 didn't feel well? [W]

2 thought the Pyramids weren't interesting? [ ]

3 played sport with other children? [ ]

4 enjoyed the meals? [ ]

5 liked an animal? [ ]

Vocabulary

Choose the correct answers.

1 This plane takes one hundred ______ .
 a neighbours
 (b) passengers

2 The ______ of this film is very famous.
 a audience
 b director

3 Charlie's dream is to fly in a hot air ______ .
 a balloon
 b basket

4 The train arrived at the ______ at 6 o'clock.
 a passport
 b platform

5 One day I want to be an actor in a famous ______ .
 a film
 b shirt

6 We saw the amazing Pyramids in the Egyptian ______ .
 a field
 b desert

7 ______ aren't very friendly animals.
 a Camels
 b Flights

8 I like ______ because they make me laugh.
 a comedies
 b dramas

9 We stayed in a lovely room in a new ______ .
 a tent
 b hotel

10 Can you carry these maps in your ______?
 a ticket
 b rucksack

11 The actor is getting ready in his ______ room.
 a expensive
 b dressing

12 The tourists visited many ______ places on their holiday.
 a interesting
 b nervous

Grammar

Choose the correct answers.

1 I didn't ______ my big suitcase on holiday.
 (a) take
 b took

2 She ______ happy when she lost her passport.
 a weren't
 b wasn't

3 When ______ you arrive at the hotel?
 a did
 b arrived

4 'Did you see the adventure film?' 'No, I ______ .'
 a wasn't
 b didn't

5 William and I ______ on the same plane to Amman.
 a was
 b were

6 Harriet didn't ______ the bus stop.
 a see
 b saw

7 Where ______ the hotel you stayed at?
 a did
 b was

8 Brian didn't visit Japan ______ year.
 a last
 b ago

9 John ______ at the station early.
 a arrived
 b arrive

10 The singer ______ me an autograph.
 a gave
 b giving

11 The flight to Rome ______ late.
 a was
 b did

12 ______ you try the food in France?
 a Did
 b Ate

Vocabulary

A Complete the table with these words.

bat butterfly dolphin eagle leopard lizard shark whale worm

Land	Air	Water
leopard		

B Write the missing letters.

1 This helps you see when it's dark. t o r c h
2 You feel like this when you need to sleep. t _ _ _ _
3 You use these to see things far away. b _ _ _ _ _ _ _ _ _
4 This is the opposite of long. s _ _ _ _
5 They fly in the sky. b _ _ _ _
6 They have six legs and some people don't like them. i _ _ _ _ _ _

C Complete the paragraph with these words.

caves dangerous dark path strong ugly

Last weekend we visited some (1) caves . We climbed down many metres. It was (2) ________, but we had a torch. We walked along a (3) ________ for about five minutes, but it was (4) ________ and Mum fell over. Dad helped her after that. He is (5) ________! Then I thought I saw a snake and I was really scared. My brother laughed because it was only a lizard. He said it was beautiful, but I thought it was (6) ________ .

Grammar

A Complete the table.

Adjective	Comparative
bad	worse
beautiful	
big	
good	
many / much	
nice	
pretty	
tall	

B Circle the correct words.

1 Crocodiles are more long / longer than lizards.
2 My dog is bigger than / bigger your dog.
3 Sharks are dangerous / more dangerous than whales.
4 Are butterflies pretty / prettier than other insects?
5 Are leopards faster / more faster than lions?
6 Mum thinks small animals are good / better than big animals as pets.

C Look at the pictures and write sentences. Use the comparative form of the adjectives.

1 elephant / strong / bird
The elephant is stronger than the bird.

4 horse / fast / turtle
____

2 bats / ugly / eagle
____

5 Katy / short / dog
____

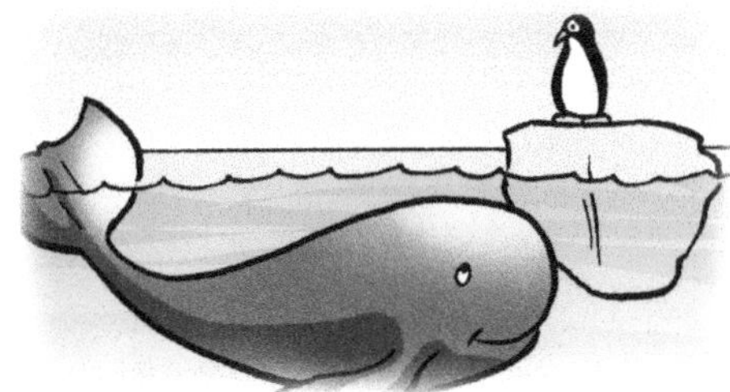

3 whale / big / penguin
____

6 cat / hungry / mouse
____

11 Lesson 2

Vocabulary

A **Complete the crossword.**

Across

B **Complete the sentences with these words.**

bring get have got love serve tear

1 My parents __________ animals and we've got three cats.
2 My sisters and I __________ the most pets in the neighbourhood.
3 Let's __________ chocolate cake at the party.
4 Dad said he can __________ me some books tomorrow.
5 I fall over a lot and I usually __________ my trousers!
6 Did you __________ a letter from Grandma?

C **Circle the odd one out.**

1	fan	cat	dog
2	sculpture	son	daughter
3	unusual	strange	important
4	diplomat	visitor	president
5	biscuits	trousers	trainers
6	lift	desk	stairs

Grammar

A **Complete the table.**

Adjective	Superlative
bad	the worst
big	______
good	______
interesting	______
nice	______
pretty	______
tall	______
many/much	______

B **Complete the paragraph with the superlative form of the adjectives in brackets.**

Film star pets

There are many famous pets in films. For me, (1) the funniest (funny) cat is Garfield. He is also (2) ______ (naughty) cat in the world! My favourite dog is Lassie. When you need help, Lassie is there. A dog like Lassie is (3) ______ (good) dog anyone can have. Another great dog is Tramp in the Disney film *Lady and the Tramp*. He is (4) ______ (bad) dog in town, but he makes friends with Lady and he becomes good. Finally, let's not forget Donkey, Shrek's talking friend in the *Shrek* films. Donkey is (5) ______ (nice) animal. He is very silly but he always tries to help Shrek. Donkey is (6) ______ (interesting) character of all because he is funny and has a famous actor's voice in the films.

C **Answer the questions.**

1 Who's the youngest person in your family? ______
2 What's the best animal for you? ______
3 What's the worst animal for you? ______
4 Where's the nicest place in your country? ______
5 Which is the most boring day of the week? ______
6 Which is the most exciting day of the week? ______

Vocabulary

Choose the correct answers.

1 My dog can do clever ______ .
  a animals
  (b) tricks

2 The ______ cat is eating the dog's dinner!
  a naughty
  b sick

3 I like horses very ______ .
  a many
  b much

4 We went to see the lions at the ______ yesterday.
  a Indonesia
  b zoo

5 The dog always waits at the ______ gate for a walk.
  a front
  b lucky

6 Can I take this cat ______, please?
  a garden
  b home

Grammar

Look at the picture and write T (true) or F (false).

1 The cat is bigger than the mouse. F
2 The crocodile is the happiest animal. ☐
3 The mouse has got the smallest ears. ☐
4 The cat is more scared than the mouse. ☐
5 The frog has got the biggest teeth. ☐
6 The frog has got the shortest legs. ☐

Say it like this!

Complete the sentences with these words.

beautiful clever funny horrible ugly

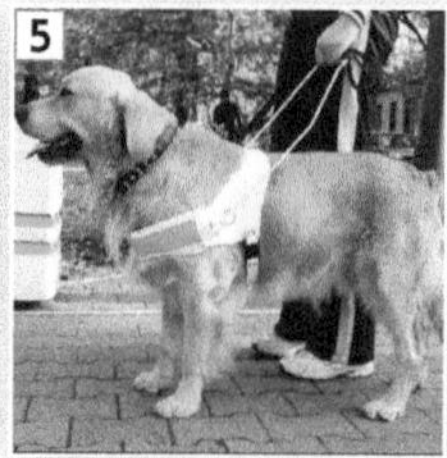

1 What beautiful parrots!
2 What a(n) ______________ cat!
3 What a(n) ______________ lizard!
4 What a(n) ______________ snake!
5 What a(n) ______________ dog!

Writing

A **Correct the spelling mistakes.**

My favourite animal

My favourite animol is the horse. Horses are strong and beatiful. They run very fast. They are usualy brown, black or white. Horses eat grass. They live for about 25 yeers. Horses spend a lot of time with peope. They are very frendly. They help people in the fields and they are also champions in competitions.

B **Write about your favourite animal. Use the plan to help you.**

Answer the questions:
What's your favourite animal?
What are they like?
What colour are they?
What do they eat?
How long do they live?
Are they friendly with people?

Vocabulary

A Write the missing letters.

1 These are white things in the sky. c l o u d s
2 You can climb on these at the beach. r _ _ _ _
3 This is often made of gold and it is beautiful. m _ _ _ _ _ _ _ _ _
4 You wear this in the rain. r _ _ _ _ _ _ _
5 You can see this in the sky when there is sun and rain at the same time. r _ _ _ _ _ _
6 You put things in these. b _ _ _ _

B Find and write six weather words.

S	U	N	N	Y	O	D	C	B
N	C	U	A	I	F	P	L	O
O	L	A	R	D	O	C	O	F
W	K	S	A	O	G	W	U	N
Y	A	B	I	F	G	I	D	W
A	F	G	N	G	Y	S	Y	E
I	C	L	Y	S	N	O	R	A
W	I	N	D	Y	L	F	V	J

1 sunny
2 ______
3 ______
4 ______
5 ______
6 ______

C Complete the sentences with these words.

have know look open rain see ~~switch on~~ take

1 Switch on the torch when we get inside the cave.
2 It's very dark in here and I can't ______ anything.
3 I've lost my cat. Can you help me ______ for her?
4 I'm sorry, but I don't ______ the answer.
5 The weather was good and luckily it didn't ______ .
6 I'm thirsty, but I can't ______ this bottle of water.
7 Let's ______ the dog to the park.
8 Did you ______ a good summer?

Grammar

A **Circle the correct words.**

Tomorrow is Saturday and it is going (1) rain / to rain, so I'm not (2) go / going to go to the park. Dad and Mum (3) are going / is going to stay at home too, so we're (4) going / are going to play some board games indoors. Dad isn't going to (5) win / winning because he always loses! Mum is a better player, but she's going to (6) lost / lose in the end because I'm the best player in the family! Well, I hope I am!

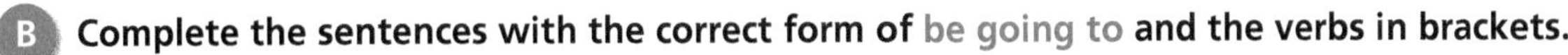

B **Complete the sentences with the correct form of be going to and the verbs in brackets.**

1 This summer it ___is going to be___ (be) really hot and sunny.
2 ____________ you ____________ (take) a raincoat with you?
3 They ____________ (not go) out in the cold weather.
4 ____________ she ____________ (look for) her umbrella in the morning?
5 I ____________ (not drive) because it's foggy.
6 We ____________ (lose) our hats because it's a really windy day!

C **Match.**

1	Are we going to eat outside?	a	No, he isn't.
2	Is Jack going to take the baby out?	b	Yes, she is.
3	Is Sandra going to wear her raincoat?	c	Yes, we are.
4	Is it going to rain?	d	Yes, they are.
5	Are they going to find the parrot?	e	No, I'm not.
6	Are you going to do your homework on Friday?	f	Yes, it is.

Vocabulary

A Put the letters in the correct order and write the landscapes.

1 flicf ___cliff___
2 stofer ______
3 lawretalf ______
4 necao ______
5 yancon ______
6 timonaun ______

B Choose the correct answers.

1 It's bad to ______ trees in the forest.
   (a) cut down
   b sell
2 We walked all day on ______ .
   a danger
   b foot
3 In the rainforests, different kinds of animals can ______ .
   a arrive
   b survive
4 I hope large companies don't ______ nature.
   a carry
   b destroy
5 The group walked for 200 ______ .
   a kilometres
   b footsteps
6 They use trees and make things out of ______ .
   a wood
   b information
7 They made a dangerous ______ through the rainforest.
   a journey
   b medicine
8 There are many ______ animals in the rainforest .
   a outdoor
   b wild

C Match.

1	Atlantic	a	park
2	nature	b	Ocean
3	hot	c	weather
4	wild	d	activities
5	outdoor	e	animal

Grammar

A **Complete the sentences with will or won't.**

1 Mum __won't__ be happy because you cut down her favourite tree.
2 The weather ________ be nice tomorrow so we can go to the beach.
3 I love nature and I hope the rainforests ________ survive.
4 We ________ stay in tents because there isn't a hotel in the forest.
5 They ________ drive on the island because there aren't any roads.
6 Tina ________ come to school tomorrow because she's sick.

B **Put the words in the correct order to make sentences and questions.**

1 ? / survive / they / will / journey / the
__Will they survive the journey?__
2 information / team / will / the / find / lots of
____
3 garden / destroy / the / dog / won't / the
____
4 rucksack / will / Dr Kay / a / carry
____
5 ? / trees / cut down / companies / will
____
6 the / tomorrow / be / won't / weather / foggy
____

C **Look at the weather for the week and answer the questions.**

Monday	Tuesday	Wednesday	Thursday	Friday	Saturday	Sunday

1 What will the weather be like on Monday? __It will be sunny.__
2 Will it be cloudy on Saturday? ________
3 What will the weather be like on Friday? ________
4 Will it be rainy on Tuesday? ________

5 Will it snow on Wednesday? ________
6 What will the weather be like on Thursday? ________

Vocabulary

Circle the correct words.

One day last year, a tornado destroyed my house. There was a (1) strong / long wind so I looked outside and I saw a very (2) scary / scared thing. 'Mum!', I shouted. 'There's a tornado and it's (3) coming towards / falling off us!' We hid in the bathroom. Dad wanted to (4) follow / take a photograph, but the tornado got very close to the house so he hid in the bathroom too. Suddenly, the tornado lifted the house (5) of / off the ground. It threw it into a field near our house. We then ran to our car and Dad (6) walked / drove away fast! We were all OK in the end!

Say it like this!

Complete the dialogue with these words.

like sunny weather wet winter

Bob: Hello?
Kate: Hi, Bob! Can you hear me? It's me.
Bob: Hi, Kate! How's Moscow?
Kate: Moscow is beautiful but the (1) weather is not that great.
Bob: What's the weather (2) __________ today?
Kate: It's cold and (3) __________!
Bob: Oh no! Have you got an umbrella with you?
Kate: Yes, I have. They said the weather's going to be better tomorrow. It's going to be (4) __________, but still very cold. It's always very cold in Moscow in (5) __________, but I've got warm clothes too, so I'm OK.
Bob: That's good. Do you want to speak to Mum and Dad?
Kate: Yes, please. Are they there?
Bob: Yes, just a minute ...

Speaking

Tell your partner how you feel about tornados.
Do you know any interesting stories?

Writing

Remember!
Always check the punctuation, grammar, spelling and word order in your writing.

A **Correct the mistakes in the story.**

It was Satorday morning and I was in the park with my brother and sister. Suddenly, it got very cloudy and started it to rain. We got very wet? We run home and took off our wet clothes. Mum gave us dry clothes and hot drinks. It rained all day and the water came the house in! Everything got wet and Mum and Dad wasn't happy! we were very scared. The rain stoped the next day.

B **Write a story about bad weather. Use the plan to help you.**

Answer the questions:
Where/When did the story happen?
What happened?
What did your mum/dad/friend(s) do?
How did you feel?

Review 6

Reading

A **Read about snakes.**

There are more than 2500 kinds of snakes. You can find them all over the world. They live in forests, rivers and even in caves.

Lots of people are scared of snakes, but snakes don't usually attack people. When snakes feel danger, they try to scare you. The American rattle snake makes a noise with its tail. The Indian cobra lifts up its head. But most snakes hide when they feel that they are in danger. They bite because they can't escape.

Snake bites aren't nice. You usually need medicine to get better. The most dangerous snake in Australia is the Brown snake. Its bite can kill you in a few minutes.

Snakes eat little things like birds, lizards, fish and insects. Big snakes don't eat often. They can wait for days or weeks for a meal.

Lots of people hate snakes, but some people love them. They like their beautiful colours and they even have pet snakes in their house.

B **Circle the correct words.**

1 There are / aren't many snakes in many countries.
2 American rattle snakes scare people with their heads / tails.
3 Brown snakes live in India / Australia.
4 Snakes eat plants / animals.
5 Some people think snakes are beautiful / little.

Vocabulary

Choose the correct answers.

1 Don't swim in the river because there are ______ in it.
a kittens
(b) crocodiles

2 Look at that beautiful ______ in the sky.
a rainbow
b rainforest

3 The ______ destroyed many houses and farms.
a tornado
b torch

4 We found the missing box in a ______ .
a cave
b rock

5 Many animals don't ______ the very cold winters.
a carry
b survive

6 The mountains are a ______ place for skiing holidays.
a popular
b rainy

7 This ______ goes through the forest and comes out at the sea.
a plant
b path

8 Don't step on a ______ because it can bite.
a parrot
b snake

9 Wear a ______ because it's going to rain.
a medallion
b raincoat

10 ______ are very clever animals.
a Butterflies
b Dolphins

11 Let's look ______ unusual flowers.
a for
b on

12 We ______ on the TV to see the news about the forest fire.
a switched
b cut

Grammar

Choose the correct answers.

1 We are ______ to see a waterfall tomorrow.
a go
(b) going

2 ______ the forest be here in fifty years?
a Will
b Going

3 Snakes are the ______ dangerous animals in this country.
a more
b most

4 Are leopards ______ than lions?
a faster
b fastest

5 Gerry is the ______ rock climber on our team.
a better
b best

6 The weather is ______ than it was yesterday.
a bad
b worse

7 Are we going ______ snakes at the zoo?
a to see
b seeing

8 Butterflies are ______ beautiful than other insects.
a more
b most

9 We hope lots of people ______ grow trees in their gardens.
a going
b will

10 Mount Everest is ______ mountain in the world.
a the higher
b the highest

11 'Is he going to cut down that tree?' 'No, he ______ .'
a won't
b isn't

12 The scientists ______ travel by car.
a isn't
b won't

Wordsearches

Units 1-2

Find these words.

amazing birthday boring clever cold comics cool family father friend fun guitar hungry laptop mother skateboard spider tall ugly young

M	O	T	H	E	R	F	S	A	N	F	S	D	L	E
Y	O	U	N	G	E	A	E	M	F	U	O	P	A	T
T	B	C	I	C	M	T	L	A	S	N	L	N	P	A
O	C	E	L	O	R	H	M	Z	K	T	A	B	T	L
A	O	S	X	L	W	E	T	I	A	Z	C	O	O	L
H	M	P	Q	D	K	R	G	N	T	R	L	R	P	A
U	I	I	L	M	L	D	U	G	E	S	E	I	F	F
N	C	U	G	L	Y	K	I	S	B	T	V	N	L	A
G	S	B	A	I	A	G	T	I	O	U	E	G	I	M
R	B	I	R	T	H	D	A	Y	A	E	R	U	O	I
Y	N	Z	R	A	C	F	R	O	R	A	O	S	B	L
F	R	I	E	N	D	S	P	I	D	E	R	R	L	Y

Units 3-4

Find these words.

bookcase carry class clean collect eat help history homework library like maths mirror need rollercoaster send sing theatre visitor wear

E	L	S	N	C	O	B	A	B	K	M	A	T	H	S
L	I	B	R	A	R	Y	B	O	S	L	N	A	F	O
M	K	D	A	R	F	L	H	O	M	E	W	O	R	K
W	E	A	R	R	A	M	S	K	B	D	C	E	O	A
X	H	R	N	Y	M	I	A	C	E	C	L	A	S	S
V	I	S	I	T	O	R	S	A	N	O	E	T	I	T
B	S	G	J	K	E	R	P	S	M	L	A	U	N	H
H	T	H	N	M	N	O	A	E	K	L	N	V	G	E
E	O	S	E	N	D	R	B	S	R	E	L	N	O	A
L	R	P	E	O	K	F	C	E	O	C	X	S	V	T
P	Y	Q	D	N	B	O	L	E	A	T	H	I	M	R
R	O	L	L	E	R	C	O	A	S	T	E	R	S	E

Units 5-6

Find these words.

cake catch cheese cook dance delicious ~~fast~~ giant hot knife
laugh make menu open play quiet rice snack throw waiter

O	K	F	A	S	T	A	O	G	I	A	N	T	B	S
M	M	T	O	N	A	L	M	F	K	K	O	P	S	T
A	L	B	P	A	N	D	E	O	N	B	C	F	D	I
K	E	G	H	C	J	A	L	P	I	O	J	K	M	J
E	P	C	E	K	S	N	W	L	F	C	A	T	C	H
M	T	S	T	L	O	C	A	K	E	H	I	H	O	K
P	V	Q	B	A	C	E	I	D	L	E	P	R	A	J
L	A	U	G	H	O	V	T	M	A	E	C	O	F	M
A	S	I	S	M	O	P	E	N	N	S	B	W	C	E
Y	N	E	C	F	K	H	R	I	C	E	H	J	F	N
H	O	T	A	B	S	F	B	L	N	I	D	B	O	U
T	S	A	E	D	E	L	I	C	I	O	U	S	B	L

Units 7-8

Find these words.

boxing ~~castle~~ champion coach cross doctor flat go kick live pilot
practise push run runner tennis train trainers trophy win

C	O	T	R	O	P	H	Y	F	L	O	N	D	S	T
A	F	T	U	N	L	O	S	P	F	A	W	O	R	K
S	D	L	N	K	K	I	T	I	H	F	I	C	K	L
T	T	E	N	N	I	S	T	L	E	O	N	T	P	S
L	R	A	E	P	C	O	R	O	L	M	S	O	C	T
E	A	U	R	S	K	L	A	T	C	P	S	R	H	F
L	I	V	E	B	D	C	I	J	R	G	F	L	A	T
O	N	W	Q	D	F	T	N	R	O	S	V	A	M	B
P	R	A	C	T	I	S	E	L	S	R	U	N	P	O
U	A	E	L	F	N	B	R	O	S	E	T	N	I	S
S	F	G	I	J	P	O	S	N	M	G	S	V	O	T
H	B	C	O	A	C	H	L	E	B	O	X	I	N	G

Wordsearches

Units 9-10

Find these words.

adventure airport comedy concert crazy director exciting famous funny camel
hotel interesting nervous plane scared ship studio suitcase thirsty travel

A	B	H	O	T	E	L	N	P	L	A	N	E	S	D
S	C	O	N	C	E	R	T	B	N	O	S	F	C	I
T	A	S	L	B	X	C	N	E	R	V	O	U	S	R
U	D	A	C	S	C	A	R	E	D	N	S	F	H	E
D	V	K	A	B	I	D	C	T	H	L	U	U	N	C
I	E	X	I	N	T	E	R	E	S	T	I	N	G	T
O	N	B	R	P	I	L	A	O	E	H	T	N	C	O
B	T	N	P	L	N	E	Z	F	J	I	C	Y	A	R
K	U	L	O	S	G	D	Y	B	C	R	A	B	M	N
E	R	A	R	B	F	A	M	O	U	S	S	L	E	G
S	E	C	T	R	A	V	E	L	F	T	E	M	L	O
S	H	I	P	S	C	O	M	E	D	Y	L	F	G	H

Units 11-12

Find these words.

bring cloud dangerous destroy dolphin eagle have important kitten know
love naughty rainbow serve short strange strong survive tired zoo

K	N	O	W	C	O	P	R	A	I	N	B	O	W	A
S	L	D	O	L	P	H	I	N	K	A	C	N	D	S
B	S	A	N	O	L	M	P	H	S	B	O	E	I	E
S	T	N	D	U	T	B	L	Z	T	M	E	N	S	R
K	O	G	E	D	I	M	P	O	R	T	A	N	T	V
I	F	E	S	N	R	O	R	O	A	B	G	A	R	E
T	T	R	T	B	E	L	S	B	N	A	L	U	O	K
T	P	O	R	T	D	N	W	S	G	T	E	G	N	F
E	O	U	O	B	R	I	N	G	E	L	V	H	G	H
N	A	S	Y	C	K	L	S	S	H	O	R	T	F	A
O	F	G	K	J	O	P	T	O	A	V	F	Y	S	V
S	U	R	V	I	V	E	Q	R	I	E	B	N	A	E

Lightning Source UK Ltd.
Milton Keynes UK
UKHW050433060822
406904UK00004B/75